There It Was, Gone

A Memoir of Childhood in the West End of Chesterfield, 1938-1955

Brian R. Ellis

20 Devonshire Street

Racecourse

O.S. Plan of West End of Newbold Moor 1919 - This map shows part of the Racecourse before its closure in 1923 to be replaced by Racecourse Road.

BABRI PUBLISHING

Internet email address: babri-publishing@hotmail.co.uk

First published in 2010
by BABRI PUBLISHING

British Library Cataloguing in Publication Data.
A catalogue record for this book is available from
the British Library.

ISBN 978-0-9564310-0-4

Printed and bound in Great Britain by
Full Point Associates Killamarsh Sheffield S21 2JU
Telephone Number 0114 251 4308

ACKNOWLEDGEMENTS

With affection to all the residents of Devonshire Street and adjacent areas of the West End without whom this book could not have been written. Also to my colleagues past and present at Whittington Engineering who shaped and moulded my future career.

My thanks to my wife Barbara with love and gratitude for her patience and understanding of my neglect of her during the preparation of this book.

I would also like to thank my brother Bernard, for his remembrances of specific names and events of these times and also giving permission to lay bare the essential facts that make this work pertinent to the time written about.

Also thanks to Marjorie Mellors and Ethel Hadfield (*nee Kennel*) for permission to use contemporary photographs.

Special thanks to Len Thompson for his many helpful suggestions and to Victoria Palfreyman for her editing of this book.

My special thanks to Simon whose faith, belief and persistence made this, and I trust further volumes in the future, possible.

I am indebted to Ordnance Survey © Crown copyright for reproducing extract from Derbyshire Sheet XV111.14. - Whittington and Newbold UD - Edition of 1919.

Finally to Dave Radford of Full Point Associates for invaluable advice and help in printing and publishing this book.

Brian R Ellis

Chesterfield 2010

LIST OF ILLUSTRATIONS

CONTENTS

INTRODUCTION

The scope of this book is to cover that period in time between 1938 and 1955. A period encompassing the Second World War, but mainly concerning when, we, as a family of four persons, lived in that part of Newbold Moor known locally as the West End and latterly the early years at New Whittington. It also covers the post war period of redevelopment and slum housing clearance programmes that would by the mid 1960's see the complete disappearance of the houses and community that was the West End, to be replaced by a wasteland of bleak concrete blocks of flats.

In writing this memoir I have tried to be entirely honest about myself, my childhood and my family. When I say in the book that I remember something, then that is the case. I do remember it. In some instances, I have relied on stories told to me by my Mum, Dad, family and friends. I hope I have separated fact from fiction, especially in the first three years of my life, having recalled these events to the best of my ability. I have made little mention of prevailing war time restrictions such as food and clothes rationing, which of course, was the case. These impositions applied generally. I wanted to be more specific.

My earliest memories begin to clarify when I was nearly three years old. Rather late, I think. The circumstances of my birth may, or may not, have hindered my cognitive thought process. Certainly, the onset of my toddler stage was delayed somewhat by the cerebral palsy condition contracted at birth. My later memories may not be absolutely perfect, historically, as like all children dates were not important to me at that time

In areas such as the West End children where traditionally free to 'play out' in the streets for long periods of time without parental supervision. It should not be surprising then that typical localities like Devonshire Street were we lived, which had many fathers away at war, made children's supervision even more problematic. There was also a climate of promiscuity engendered by those unnatural times of prolonged separation. Many exploits referred to in this book were pursued without malice of fore thought and practiced without parental knowledge or approval.

My mother's family were wealthier than my father's. Descendants of journeymen tradesmen, they had newly acquired wealth through the proceeds of their business of motor car dealers. My father's family were lower working class, but had about them a generosity of soul, that only the experience of poverty could foster.

I came from one particular place, and time. And one particular family, and belong to both. For which I feel truly blessed.

When you walk into your memories, you are opening a door to the past, the road within has many branches and the route is different every time. Necessarily therefore this memoir does not read as a seamless journey and trust that my many digressions do not disrupt the essential continuity.

The book was written with the best of intentions, so please forgive any offence caused by what I have either included or omitted... certainly none was intended.

PROLOGUE

I've watched you now a full half hour,

Self-poised upon that yellow flower;

A little Butterfly! Indeed

I know not if you sleep or feed.

WILLIAM WORDSWORTH

The world revolved around his pram. The daily journey from starkly furnished kitchen, through cobbled yard to jennel that tunnel of semi-darkness that reeked of damp. Then out again into street of drab red brick terrace, smut and grime covered under umbrella's cloudy sky. Then upwards, now passing grey washed houses with vestige of cultivation swamped by weeds. Now crossing a road and down the path to a door. Journeys end, another kitchen, another long day to sit in the pram. It's now dark outside, lights blacked out. A chill air whose breath that freezes hands and face. At last, the sanctuary of his stark grey kitchen again. Now the nightly ritual begins. He is stood on the scrubbed down table and the plaster bandages are ripped from his feeble lower limbs. He screams against unbearable pain. The stench of germolene pervades his brain. When will this nightmare end?

The same mind dulling journey again and again. Yet today was different. Nin gave him a present, a wonderful present that danced and shimmered in the morning light. All day he looked and stared with wonderment at the beautiful sight, the shapes so silver bright seeming to dance in sheer delight. The precious jar was transported back and placed upon the shelf above the pram. Yes safe and sound till morning came. Then, in a flash the spectre sprang upon the infant in his pram, spilling the jar from shelf to floor. Alas! They danced no more. The infant cried and cried and mourned the loss. But still that night the plaster bandages where torn, and the infant cried till dawn. At last this nightly ritual ended, the bandages replaced by rods of steel, which formed a cage around those feeble limbs, and still he was a prisoner of that pram.

Then on a sunny afternoon he cast his shackles, and was free. No more rods of steel no more bended knees, no more sitting in that pram. With fortitude he boldly strode across those cursed cobbled stones. Behold, as if decreed by fate, before his eyes a magical place, a garden to delight his soul. Before him a tunnel of poles with leaves and flowers intertwined. And settled upon this foliage of green and red, a butterfly, wings out spread, with coloured hues of russet browns and blues, as if displayed for him to view.

How had this magical place appeared to him?

This was in the summer of 1940.

Chapter 1 – Devonshire Street

I will arise and go now, and go to Innisfree

And a small cabin build there, of clay and wattles made.

WILLIAM BUTLER YATES

The Lake Isle of Innisfree

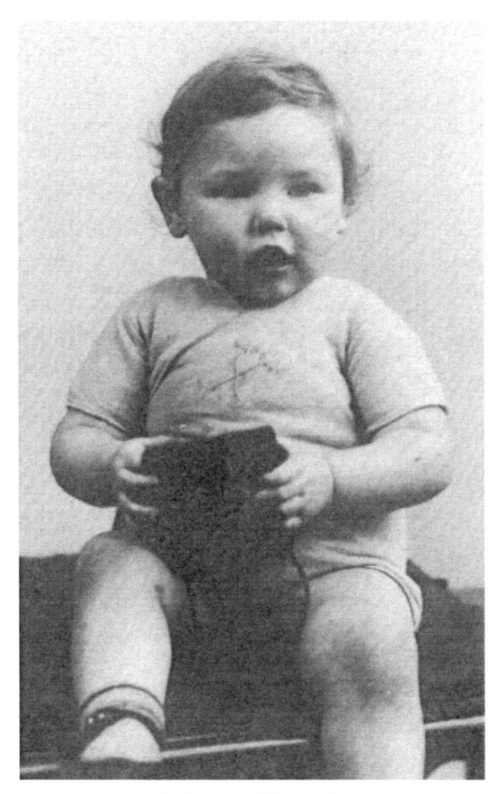

Author age 12 months

'Are kid ulldo it.' I was just turned four years old at that time in 1942 when these words were spoken by my elder brother to Blood Jones one Sunday afternoon outside of Jacky Tucker's shop on the bottom of the West End. Jacky's surname was Huckerby but for reasons unknown to me everybody called him Tucker. Outside of Tucker's shop was a place were the other kids from the West End would meet up to talk, or to play a street game. Generally though we kids from Devonshire Street would only occasionally go on the bottom rather preferring to stay in our own street.

I had on occasion seen Blood Jones knocking about the bottom, never dare speaking to him.

I viewed him with complete awe. For, had not our Bernard told me wonderful tales about this most unusual character who at the age of fifteen had run away from home and now some two years later was living all alone in a hole in the brook's bank side and snared rabbits and caught fish? I think everybody held him in awe for he had an uncanny aura about him than generated admiration and respect at first meeting.

It seemed like every kid from the West End had gathered by the brook side that afternoon to witness Blood climb up to a tree pippet's nest hole in the top of an Elm tree with me sat precariously on his shoulders. Blood had discovered this nest site but could not get his hand down the hole sufficient to reach the eggs even when using a spoon tied to a stick. Blood had come on to the bottom to seek out a small child who would be able to reach the eggs. Our Bernard put me forward. Always he was the one with bravado but for this challenge he was too big. 'Are you up for it *Titch*.' Blood asked me. I was dumfounded that Blood had actually addressed me and could only muster a nod in reply. Our Bernard told me recently that whilst I was in the tree his heart was in his mouth, and kept thinking 'If anything should happen what I will tell Mam.' This was a really proud moment and in my childish naivety I must admit an element of showing off to the encircled crowd. Maybe the expectation was that Blood might let me fall but it never crossed my mind that there was any danger as I had complete faith in this Pied Piper of the West End.

Blood was up that tree in a trice. I could reach an egg using the spoon but it would tantalisingly slip off the spoon just as I was about to clear the hole. 'Try and take off thee jumper.' Blood said. I tried to peel it off from the front but couldn't get it up and passed Blood's head. I then leaned backwards and tried to pull it over my head but it got jammed on my head. I couldn't see a bloody thing. With the jumper still stuck over my head and me half strangling Blood we made it back to the ground were I was stripped to the waist and once again we went back up to the nest hole. As I pushed my arm down into the hole I could feel a number of eggs but could only use two fingers to gentle lift them out of the nest. Each one was placed into Bloods mouth, apparently a total of five eggs in all. On return to the ground I felt euphoric. My reward was a small off-white egg streaked with purple markings. I did not realise at that moment that I had gained street credibility that would prove to be a cross to bear during my primary schooling. I had also gained a nickname *Titch* which everybody called me henceforth.

Blood was independently minded and survived in his hole for over a further year. Once at his invitation I visited him at this location and to my young mind it was impressively comfortable. The walls were lined out in clay and it had a fire hole and chimney. During these times he would always make a fuss of me when he put in an occasional appearance on the bottom of the West End. Finally he left the area to join the armed forces. I never saw him again.

The unrestricted freedom of me being at the top of a tree at four years old was only made possible by being raised in a cultural world of a working class districts, such as the West End, where children were traditionally allowed to 'play out' in the streets for long periods of time without supervision. The fabric of the West End was demolished in the 1960s as part of the slum clearance program and along with it was destroyed the very essence of the spirit of communal living that is now just a fond nostalgic memory to many of those who are fortunate to have been brought up in such an area at that period of time.

The West End was the local name given to an area within the parish of Newbold Moor, Chesterfield. It had no visible boundaries, but consensus opinion was that it was centred about Devonshire Street and Arundel Road, laying parallel to one another. It also included the part of Mountcastle Street, which ran across the bottom of both others. Newbold Moor and Whittington Moor were communities encircled by the Chesterfield Racecourse up to the middle of the 1920's when it was redeveloped into housing by the borough council. The West End was an isolated enclave lying outside the racecourse and was linked to Newbold Moor by its only approach, Mountcastle Street which crossed over the western end of the racecourse. In the early twentieth century the West End had a reputation as being the toughest neighbourhood in the parish, and arguably, in the entire borough of Chesterfield It was definitely a *no go* area if you did not need to visit there. Local folklore's superstition was that neighbouring localities interpreted the area not as the geographic West End, but *Worse End*, the grammatical intent as in their local dialect syntax, i.e. 'It was the *west* thing I ever did.' The fact that the area is geographically situated on the west side of Newbold Moor is the more probable answer

Typical inhabitants of the West End in the 1920's where 'Crutchie' Lister and Corker Hardy, two young tearaways with no respect for law and order. In one altercation they had assaulted the person of Constable Ullathorne the incumbent Barlow Village police officer during his attempt to arrest them for poaching. It was alleged that Lister had used his crutch to knock the constable to the floor and Hardy had then kicked him with savage violence. My great uncle George Edward a.k.a. Crutchie told me that Ullathorne had on previous occasions 'done' them for trifling incidents resulting in him and Corker eventually being sent to Borstal. He had sworn that one day he would put them away for good. George Edward told me that on the night of the assault six of them from the West End including my grandfather Walter Hardy, elder brother of Corker, had been netting rabbits in Haslam's field at Cutthorpe when Ullathorne was spotted approaching on his bike. 'The bugger was on his own so it would be his word against ours.' George Edward said. 'We left the nets and were going through the main road gate when Ullathorne started blowing his whistle. I downed him with me crutch and Corker started in to him just as Farmer Haslam came out to see what the ruckus was about and he saw me and Corker. The rest had got away.' The two of them were imprisoned for a term of six months hard labour.

As George Edward put it 'We ended up doin time and sewing mail bags I ort to have killed that swine Ullathorne.' It seems ironical that some ten years later George Edward and Walter Hardy were pillars of the community being respected motor car traders thank to the business savvy of Bernard Lister eldest brother of George Edward and brother-in-law to Walter Hardy.

At the time of my birth my parents Hilda and Walter Ellis together with their eighteen month old son Bernard were currently lodging in one room at 14 Manknell Road, a house tenanted by Walter's parents with four of their children. The overcrowded conditions prevented privacy and decency, in every respect. Hilda, in particular was subject to constant embarrassment with constant violation of their small space. A nine hour exhausting labour added pressure into this intolerable stressful cauldron when I was born at ten minutes past four in the early morning of Friday the 4th February 1938 and was duly christened Brian Rodger Ellis. I was born with

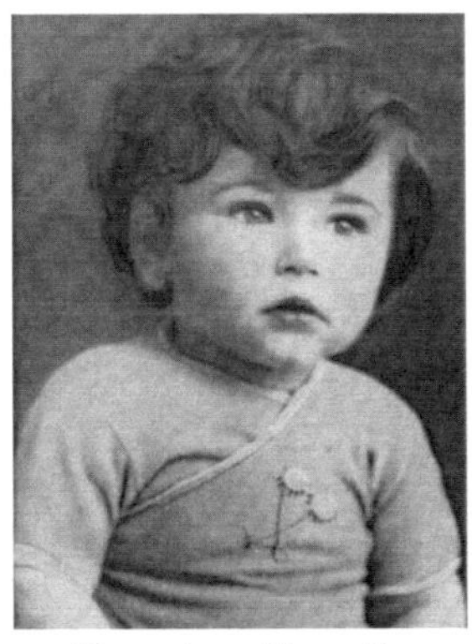

Bernard age 18 months

a congenital weakness of my lower limbs a condition that ran through the Lister branch of our family with my uncle, great uncle and several second cousins being afflicted with the same condition. In an attempt to alleviate this condition Mum had to strap my legs in plaster bandages at weekly intervals for two years. Mum used to smear my legs with germolene ointment before applying the bandages to act as a releasing agent but removal always caused me terrible pain. I was confined to a pram for two years and Mum also had to use the pram for me on longish journeys such as shopping for the next two years.

A short time after my birth there was an improvement in income and living conditions, as my Dad was re-employed by B R Mills as a lorry driver and we moved into a house with sole occupation. It transpired, that in the late spring of 1938 due to the overcrowding conditions prevailing at Manknell Road, my Mum and Dad had been offered the tenancy of a local authority owned semi-detached house on Racecourse Road. For reasons that I was not privy to, my maternal grandparents took the tenancy, and we ended up renting the house just vacated by them. It was alleged that money changed hands as a bribery to persuade Mum and Dad to relinquish their option. The more plausible explanation is that my grandparents had genuine need to move away from their own overcrowding at Devonshire Street, hence, the councils readily acceptance of exchange and of course Mum and Dad would pay a substantially lower rent by moving to the West End. Certainly by late 1938 the West End was a rundown slum area with substandard housing and lacked amities at the time that we, as a family of four moved into number 20 Devonshire Street. (See appendix 1 for early family history).

The house was a two up, two down terrace. Accommodation actually consisted of a front living room, rear kitchen, two bedrooms, cellar and outside closet forming part of the rear garden boundary wall some twenty yards from the house.

These are the bare facts about the house. To give the reader a sense of what was the reality, it is necessary to describe the house and locale as it appeared in the time of my own early memory of it, sometime in 1942;

The living room which measured ten feet by ten feet had an entrance door that opened directly from the outside pavement. A single glazed sash opening window gave view onto the street. This room was dominated by a cast iron Victorian Yorkshire Range which featured a combination of boiler, fire opening and oven, all surmounted by an over mantle on which reposed a Smiths wind up clock, salvaged from a motor car that was housed in an arts and craft style oak case. From the ceiling there hung a bayonet type single electric light fitting with exposed bulb. Other features were recessed cupboards either side of range, and a door that lead directly into the kitchen. Furnishings were very basic due to an acute lack of space, but included, a small oak dining table, two hand painted chairs, a two seat settee, which sat tightly between table and rear wall and a 'what not' plant stand that supported the all important Bush radio. The floor was covered by cheap, oil based linoleum, which crazed and fragmented during hot weather giving off a not too unpleasant odour. The only concession to comfort was a home made pegged hearth rug.

Passing directly through to the kitchen the cellar head, which served as a larder, was on the immediate right. To the left was a small, whitewood scrubbed top table used for baking and food preparation, and next to this, a blue vitreous enamel gas cooking stove. At far left was a built in coal fired copper. A stoneware sink with a single cold water tap, situated beneath the rear widow, completed the sparse fixtures and fittings. The kitchen served also for the parking of my green coloured low slung pram, beneath a make shift shelf.

The cellar head contained a *cold slab*, a stone shelf for keeping perishable food cool. There were no white goods back then which usually meant shopping on a daily basis for perishables. Under the slab reposed an enamel bucket with a heavy stone on top, It was perpetually used for pressing oxen tong in salt brine. The cellar head also stored the *dolly-tub* and other accoutrements used for wash day.

The stair case was near the back kitchen door and lead up to two bedrooms. The front bedroom had a small Victorian cast iron fireplace as its only feature. The rear bedroom again was sparse, having a large wall cupboard that served as a *glory hole*

The cupboard gave access to the roof space, which some eight years later would provide an amusing episode. This will be discussed in more detail later in the book.

The kitchen back door opened on to a cobbled yard that served as a right of way to neighbouring properties. The yard housed a cumbersome mangle protected from the weather by a tarpaulin. The outside wall had a galvanised steel bath hanging on it. Across the yard was the slightly elevated garden with a central pathway that led to the closet and brick boundary wall. Beyond the wall, straight ahead were rough pastoral grass lands and hedgerows that stretched into the far distance toward Dunston Lane and bordered to the right by Ridding Brook, a small stream that flowed into the river Whiting at Old Whittington. These fields and the brook bottom would become our very own adventure playground for several years.

This house was our very first family home. My Mum was very house proud keeping it spick and span. When Dad came home from work he was not allowed in the living room before he had washed and changed out of his working clothes. Likewise with me and Bernard when as likely as not we would arrive home wet and muddy. Mum had a weekly routine like most of our neighbour's. Monday was wash day. Early she would light a fire under the copper to heat up the water in which she would then boil the items. She would then transfer a portion of the wash to the dolly tub were she would agitate them with her dolly. This was a heavy wooden pole with a cross bar handle at its top and attached to its bottom was a disc with three short legs attached. This cumbersome device was turned to and fro in the washing. She would then press the washing up and down using her ponch. The items would be scrubbed on her rubbing board and finally rinsed under the cold water tap. Mum would then take separate items into the yard and remove surplus water by passing them through her large roller mangle prior to hanging them out to dry on the garden clothes line or hung over the fire guard in bad weather. Once the items were damp dry Mum would then iron them using one of the two flat Iron's that had to be heated on the fire grate. The very iron's that now reposes in my fireplace. Tuesdays and Fridays Mum worked for her mother doing cleaning and domestic chores. Wednesday Mum would clean the house from top to bottom, changing all the bedding, blackleading the Yorkshire range and donkey stoning the front and rear window sills and door steps Saturday was baking day mainly bread and currant teacakes. When making pastries I would assist with rolling out the dough, cutting the shapes and placing them in the baking trays and finally putting the filling in.

Sunday was the only day of the week that the family sat down together. Breakfast was a fry up with dried egg, tin tomatoes and fried spam. Mum would always prepare a full roast beef or pork dinner, together with Roly poly jam roll. Alternatives would be Steam treacle or Spotted dick puddings. Fortunately, Dad delivered meat to local butchers throughout the period of the Second World War so we were never short of meat. I especially like what was called pork sweetmeats which came wrapped in greaseproof paper which I tried to use as drawing paper. After dinner Mum and Dad would retire to bed in the afternoon for a well earned rest whilst Bern and I would play out either in the street or on the back yard. Sunday teatime was special for me as we would have my favourite homemade bread and dripping with salt followed by jelly or pink blancmange. On occasions we had a special treat of ox tongue either served with a salad or made into sandwiches and spread with Branson's mixed pickle or piccalilli. Mums bread 'n' drip would attract most of the streets kids and particularly Leonard *Monk* Sims from off Racecourse Mount. During teatime Monk would press his face close up to the window and of course would be invited in to join us. Roger Huckerby or Peter Wright, or both, would also put in an appearance and stand at the table drinking tea, each with a doorstop sandwich stuck in their hands. In the evening Mum would arrange for a neighbour's daughter Lilly Umney to baby sit me whilst she and Dad went down to the Railway Hotel, a public house on Whittington Moor. Our Bern would be out on the street with his pal Ronnie Huckerby, cousin to Roger. When Mum and Dad came back from the pub at about 10.30pm Mum would make a fry up bubble and squeak from the dinner left over. This would be sprinkled liberally with Daddies brown sauce. In the week Mum would serve up Meat and tatie pie, Steak and kidney pud, Tatie hash and my favourite Stew and dumplings. When I was poorly or 'off the hooks' as we would say Mum would give me fresh sliced tomato in malt vinegar seasoned with salt and pepper. I still to this day relish this concoction when I'm off the hooks it seems to work wonder's.

Dad became a proficient vegetable gardener, adhering to the Ministry of Information poster slogan urging you to *Dig for Victory*. Dad was also a dab hand at maintenance and turned the outside lavatory into a little heaven on earth. All the pipes were lagged against freezing using strips of Hessian sacking. The wooden door had strips of rubberised conveyor belting nailed to all the edges as draft excluders. The inside was whitewashed and for night time use there was provided an hurricane type paraffin lamp which when lit gave of a warm cosy glow with an intoxicating aroma that would keep our Bern on the *dunacon* for what seemed to me forever while he read his comics.

Our house was situated half way up the street on the right. The houses on this side were identical there being a string of five terrace houses before a break gave way to rough ground on which stood Johnny Martin's deep litter hen coups and Harrison's builder's yard. The terrace then continued to the street top, where on either side of the street were enclosed yards. On the right lived the

Bargh and Bunting families. The left yard was occupied by the Brittain and Sylvester families. On the left side of the street there was a continuous row of terrace housing. These houses were slightly bigger than ours having a living kitchen. Their front rooms were only used for high days and holidays. This I could never understand and even though not being used the curtains were drawn out of respect when a funeral cortège was to pass by. The terraces where interspersed with tunnel ways, called jennels, which gave back access to blocks of six houses, all having right of way across each others property. All front doors had access directly off the pavement.

A third of the way up was Mrs Grubb's shop, being the front room of her house which on entry always smelled pungently of camphor, the chemical used for manufacture of moth balls which were always in stock. I never knew how she managed to make a living as the dimly lit room was barely furnished with a few plank shelves on which was staked cartons of Birds custard powder, a few bottles of lemonade, flour and self raising flower, and her allotted twelve 4d loaves, the *standard white loaf* introduced by the government as the basic staple food. Mum would make me wait outside of our house to catch sight of the bread delivery van and then dash down to Grubb's to buys a loaf There was usually a stampede for the bread. It was not on ration but always in short supply. Mrs Grubb also stocked general haberdashery items such as needles, cotton thread, darning wool together with potions, ointments and pills for every conceivable ailment, there were Beechams cooling powders for colds and influenza. I hated these, the powder stuck to the roof of my mouth and caused my throat to constrict and heave up sick. Beechams also made blood and stomach pills to keep you regular. Dad administered them on a Sunday night after he came back from the pub. My Mum always insisted that I had a 'stuffled' or bronchial chest and would regularly administer Owbridge's Lung Tonic than had the consistency of sump oil. I kept telling her that the trouble was caused by having to breathe through my mouth, but she would have none of it. There was Vic vapour rub,

Fiery Jack another rub and Ralgex for muscle and pain relief. She also stocked home remedies like Sulphur of Molasses, Camphor Oil and Indian brandy. All of the above have been forced down my throat or rubbed onto my body at some time or other for I am sure Mum was swayed by the claims of bogus medical remedy adverts appearing in her weekly Red Letter magazine by such claims as Fight Flu with Fennings Fever Mixture and You'll Feel Better.

The 'bottom' of the West End was lower Mountcastle Street on which was situated a further three shops; Jack Slight's at the corner of Hardwick Street was a grocer and hardware shop, very similar to *Arkwright's in Open All Hours.* Whenever we entered his premises, he would rush from the living quarter into the shop to deter any temptation by us to shop lift. He always had on the same soiled brown smock and would be incessantly coughing whilst taking drags on the ever present fag which dropped fag ash everywhere, even when serving cheese or bacon. He would greet you with the disdainful remark; 'what do you want sludge?' He had a noticeable habit of keeping his left hand on the scale when weighing goods. We would often pass by his shop at night time and would stop to watch mice scampering about the shop front window. Further along Mountcastle Street Billy Huckerby had a shop either side of the corners of Arundel Road. Tucker's was a sweet shop and green grocer run by Billy's son Jacky. This was a general meeting place were 'characters' from the west end whiled away there time. On the opposite corner Billy ran a general provisions store. This shop had been previously owned by my great grandfather George Lister and in the early 1950's by Billy Kidd who had been a full back for the Chesterfield Football Club. . Opposite these two shops was a piece of waste ground on which was situated the defunct Tin Mission Hall then used as a store for Billy Huckerby's shops.

Racecourse Mount ran from the top of Devonshire Street passing the top of Arundel Road before meeting Racecourse Road at point just below were Racecourse Road crossed St Johns Road. Just over St Johns Road was 47 Racecourse Road were my maternal grandparents the Hardy's lived and was about five minutes walk from our house in Devonshire Street. In fact you could walk around the whole of the West End within ten minutes.

Chapter 2 – Junkers 88

Mild the mist upon the hill,

Telling not of storms to-morrow;

No; the day has wept its fill,

Spent its store of silent sorrow.

EMILY BRONTE

Mum, Dad & Bruce on back field at Devonshire Street 1946

As my mind scans my memory banks stored over a lifetime of some seventy years, it seems remarkable to me that my brain can instantly recall the first complete conscious vision and thought process whilst I stood in our garden at Devonshire Street on a sunny day in 1940.

Dad back garden of Devonshire Street 1947

I cannot, with certainty, pinpoint that obviously important moment in time, but place it between July and September of that glorious, long hot summer. I can speculate because there were pods and flowers on my Dad's runner bean plants. I had been irresistibly drawn to the tall row of beans by the profusion of coloured butterflies attracted to their flowers which was in stark contrast to our neighbours empty waste ground.

That defining moment in the garden was, or maybe not, inspired by a combination of factors coming together on that afternoon. Firstly the afternoon weather was pleasantly warm and sunny. Secondly the garden looked its very best. Thirdly, and most significant, I was allowed to walk a short distance unaided, which had been a rare occurrence.

That summer of 1940 was one of the hottest on record in terms of hours of sunshine, certainly helped by introducing daylight saving time. You may have heard someone say 'The days seemed to be a lot longer, when I was a child'. I have thought that myself, then, dismissing it as nostalgic memories from a carefree childhood. Well, for the duration of the Second World War, in terms of daylight time, they were, actually longer. To save energy and provide longer daylight working hours the government introduced what was called double summer time or daylight saving time. No, not time travel, but by simply advancing the clock two hours ahead of GMT instead of the usual one hour that we are familiar with. It gave kids an extra hour of playtime in summer throughout the war period.

The popular tunes of that first year of the war were at first upbeat reflecting the optimism of a quick resolution, and then they became evocative of the deep felt yearning for a return to normality as the blitz took its toll during those dark hours, with such songs as; *Run Rabbit Run, We're Gonna Hang Out the Washing on the Siegfried Line, and It's a Lovely Day Tomorrow, A Nightingale Sang in Berkeley Square*, then *We'll Meet Again*.

The blockbuster film was *The Gapes of Wrath* from a novel by John Steinbeck. Then *Waterloo Bridge* a weepy starring Robert Taylor and Vivien Leigh. More of an attraction for younger children *The Sea Hawk* a swashbuckling classic starring Errol Flynn.

On the home service of the BBC you could listen to a light entertainment offering *The Forces Program, Music While you Work* and of course the speeches of Winston Churchill and the nightly war news read by Alver Liddell or John Snagge.

My pram was a boon to Mum as she made her twice weekly journey to Racecourse road, where she was employed to cleanse her parent's house, which included scrubbing floors on her knees, for which she was paid, the paltry sum of five shillings and the occasional present of a tin or packet of foodstuff. On these occasions I was sat up, or sleeping in the pram, parked in kitchen. It was chiefly in that place, which was a thoroughfare for family, and also, many visitors, that I believe, my memories began to clarify. Shadow figures materialised, and some would become major influences, throughout my childhood and into maturity.

The most influential was my maternal grandmother who I affectionately called Nin. The other major influence was my maternal grandfather referred to as Dadad. My brother, Bern and me, at that time, where their only grand-children.

The striking thing about Nin's kitchen was the window, which was overlaid with buff coloured tape, forming a pattern of diamond shapes. Apparently, recommended as being effective in limiting spread of shattered window panes resulting from bomb blast. This was 1940 and we were at war. There was also brown paper strips, with one of their sides covered in flies, hanging from the ceiling. This was Nin's domain, holding court to a bevy of callers whilst leaning on the kitchen table, seldom entering the spacious living room until early evening. Small and rather dumpy, hair when loose hung down as far as her lower back but normally combed tightly back, terminating in a bun at the nape of the neck, characteristic plain Lister features with slight jowl and round brown eyes. She was never without her pinafore, cup of tea and woodbine cigarette, this was my Nin .To sooth her asthmatic like cough caused by heavy smoking Nin would throughout the day take a tea spoon of 'Lin Cam' a special very strong cough remedy to which she became addicted. My Nin was always available and ever dependable, hardly ever venturing past her front garden gate, other than her weekly visit to the Westminster Bank on Whittington Moor. There was one notable exception, on her fiftieth birthday in 1945, when I was seven, Nin took my Mum, other younger daughters Joan and Esme, and me to the Victoria Restaurant in Chesterfield and hosted her birthday celebratory party. A special day I have always treasured.

Dadad was born ten years before the death of Queen Victoria. In the 1940's his demeanour was a reflection of late Victorian England, being frugal and a creature of habit. In business he was astute. In recreation he was generous of hospitality and socialised with like minded males. He was of slight build with piercing grey blue eyes that together with his aquiline nose and balding head gave him a bird like appearance... In dress he was never seen without formal attire of collar, tie, and three piece business suit, over which in inclement weather he wore a Cromby overcoat and grey Harris Tweed flat cap. His shoes always polished to a mirror like finish. Every day Dadad adhered to the same ritual. Breakfast, then taken by car to his motor car sales and scrap metal business premises for a two hour period. His premises, the Yard, as it will now be called, was, and still is, situated at the corner of Dunston Road and Racecourse Road, a distance of half a mile or less from home. Return home for dinner which was generally fish or chicken. The fresh fish was brought in daily from Warner's Fishmongers in Chesterfield. Then a further two hours at the Yard before returning home again at 4pm for teatime. At 5pm, his two sons Jack and Sid would arrive from the Yard to have a meal, typical fried egg and bacon. I remember how good that cooked bacon smelt to me. Eggs and bacon were officially on ration but Nin seemed never to be short. During tea Dadad would discuss the day's business with the lads. At 5.30pm he would partake of a mixture of MacLean's stomach powder mixed with two raw eggs to soothe his ulcerated stomach. He would then retire to bed for two hours. At 8pm he would be chauffeured to the Victoria Club and Institute at Whittington Moor where he socialised with his brother in laws, the Listers, and John Madin, then in furniture retail, now in music. At 10pm chauffeured back home where he would relax with family and friends, keeping them up, usually until after midnight at which point Dadad would insist that everyone stood to attention whilst the radio played the closing national anthem. The only deviation was Sunday nights when he entertained at home usually the guests would be his two brothers in law Charlie and George Edward Lister, Jack Taylor and his wife Hilda who was Nin's younger sister and George Watterson a car salesman who worked for Cliff Machent a fellow motor trader with business at Edmund Street. Dadad and I often stood side by side with our backs towards the fireplace, and I recall one evening when we were jostling each other to get nearer the fire that Dadad repeated to me a riddle told to him at the Victoria Club, that he had failed to fathom out. The riddle went something like this:

Three men all have £10 each and needed a Radio. They went to Wards shop and asked the Assistant 'how much is that radio?' '£30' replied the Assistant. They all pay there £10 and were on there on the way with the radio. The assistant, being pleased with him self tells his Manager he has sold the radio for £30. The Manager points out that the radio was priced at £25 only, and instructs the Assistant to catch up with the three men and return the £5.The Assistant grabs five one pound notes from the till and gives chase. While on his way he realises that £5 doesn't split between three, so he gives each man a £1 back and pockets the remaining £2. Now each man as paid only £9 making a total of £27 The Assistant as pocked £2. So were has the other pound gone?

Dadad was an astute business man with a keen mind and I was mystified why, try as I may, I could not convince Dadad that there was no missing pound but to his dying day he insisted that there was, as he could nor understand, and would not accept my explanation. If the reader is also baffled do not be disheartened too much, as at first telling many, many people fail to do the sums right.

My paternal grandparents had moved to Dowdeswell Street, Chesterfield which was on a direct bus route from Racecourse Road being about four miles distant. Geographically, it could have been a million miles away as we seldom, if ever visited them until I was five years old, and then infrequently. The consequence was that I never did form a natural bond. It was no one's fault. Circumstance and easy access to Nin and Dadad's home made a certain inevitability that I would gravitate to them. Which, of course I did.

To keep me amused one afternoon in Nin's kitchen, she placed on the table in front of my pram, a large glass jam jar containing two dead sprats, floating head down in tap water.

I remember being utterly fascinated by their beautiful silver sheen. And, as Nin occasionally twisted the jar around, the fish danced in front of my eyes. They were truly alive in my mind. Later, I must have kicked up an awful fuss which served to achieve my want, as when we returned home that night, the jar of fish came with us. It was placed on a shelf in our kitchen, the pram being parked beneath. My first waking thought that next morning was of my fish, and lo and behold, there they were, and from my pram I contentedly sat transfixed as they floated serenely in their jar.

Mum & Jim back of 20 Devonshire Street 1947

As the kitchen door was opened for the first time that morning in came Jim our large black Tom cat. As was Jim's custom, having spent a night outdoors he began to prowl around the kitchen foraging for food scraps. My worse fears were realised as he took up position by my pram. The curiosity in those malevolent penetrating amber eyes betrayed his intent as they slowly moved first to the jar and then hypnotically held my gaze. Jim knew from past encounters that he could best me when it came to fending him off my food. In an instant, and like the Black Panther he was to me, Jim sprang up pinning me to the pram then used me as a bridge to the shelf and with his front paws knocked the jar to the floor where he quickly devoured the fish. He then sat by the pram like some black evil spectre contentedly licking himself. This incident was traumatising that no manner of assurances or offers of replacement could console me for weeks afterwards and is still etched in my mind to this day.

Mum & Bruce back of 20 Devonshire Street 1947

We also owned a pet dog, a small cross bread terrier named Bruce who Dadad had taken in exchange for a distributor head. I said we owned him but Bruce was a free spirit commuting between Devonshire Street, the Yard and Racecourse Road. He would often accompany me and our Bern when out on the back fields or down at the brook bottom and then would take off somewhere else as the fit would take him. Bruce lived to be well over seventeen and when we relocated from the West End to New Wittington in 1951 he came along with us and seemed content not to go roaming. Dadad would often consider anything in exchange or part exchange for car spares. In one instance he took an African Grey Parrot complete with cage. He brought the parrot home and left it in the kitchen overnight. In the morning Nin, who was oblivious of Dadad's barter came down to make their early morning tea and when she went to fill the kettle the parrot squawked 'Making a cuppa tea Ma.' Nin naturally freak out so the parrot had to find a new home.

In September my Uncle Jack, I always called him Jack, was conscripted into the armed forces. Sid was exempt as he was born with leg paralysis and wore steel callipers. Jack's entry into the army left Dadad with no one to carry out the job of scrapping cars as Sid's condition precluded his carrying out arduous work. My Mum donned boiler suit and turban to step into the breach. She had the both of us kids to consider. Bern was no problem as he attended Edmund Street infant's school, only a few yards up the road from the Yard. It was arranged that I would go to Nin in the morning and then transfer to the Yard for two hours in the afternoon as mum would leave at 3.00pm to pick up our Bern. This new commitment necessitated re-arrangement of her domestic chores, particularly the two days at my Nin's. This was solved by changing it to evening time.

Mum scrapped cars for four years until our Jack obtained a discharge from the army to carry out war surplus work at the Yard which the government designated as vital to the war effort. What transpired was that Dadad had obtained a contract with the Ministry of Defence to dispose of war surplus military vehicles by re-cycling. I remember making many trips with our Jack and Sid in the break down lorry to recover vehicles from a holding compound at the top of Glapwell hill from late 1944 to well into 1946.

These vehicles were mainly Ford saloon cars, and for a child they presented a veritable Pandora's Box of goodies. They had been used by the American Army and were crammed full of maps, army manuals, and first aid kits but most desirable, multi coloured rank and unit shoulder badges.

With the onset of autumn the clocks went back one hour, and much to the chagrin of the children of Devonshire Street, also, the blackout restrictions imposed at the outbreak of the war curtailed their night time play, centred on the streets gas lamp that remained unlit.

The year's war situation reports broadcast on the wireless by the BBC's Home Service had, for small children growing up in the West End, no relevance. They had a parochial existence, often not venturing out of their own street, other than attending school. If truth were known it had very little interest to the adult populace, other than the few whose spouse was a serviceman. It was a long way off, and therefore, remote. Even the report of the blitz of London, commencing on 7th September caused little concern. 'Did anyone know where London was?'

This indifference was soon to be questioned, if not heeded, when on the night of Thursday 12th December at 7pm; the first bombs fell on the city of Sheffield and bombing continued to 4am. The din was deafeningly audible and the incendiary bomb fires clearly visible on that clear, crisp night, to the resident of the West End, some twelve miles distant.

The bombing of Sheffield by the German Luftwaffe on the nights of 12th and 15th December 1940, was headlined in the local newspaper, The Star, as the Sheffield Blitz. This bombing focused in the mind of the populations of South Yorkshire and North Derbyshire the reality that the front line of war had moved to their own doorstep. This was now the home front.

Two weeks after the blitz I actually remember being driven through Sheffield city centre and witnessing the destruction. It was just into the New Year, our Bern was still on Christmas holiday break from school. Mum was working that morning down at the Yard.

Our Sid had to visit Bentley Brothers motor factors situated close by the Wicker Arches so he offered to take Bernard and me with him. We often accompanied him despite our Bern's habit of regularly leaning over from the back seat and covering Sid's eyes with his hands whilst Sid was driving. That morning has we entered the city the acrid smell of burning permeated thought out the car, then the still smoking ruins came into view. The image that has stuck in my mind to this day was of a bed still with bedding, tilted precariously out of all that remained of a bedroom that had its end wall blown away. Our Sid told my parents that a chap at Bentley's said 'That the destruction seemed to lie all along the tram line routes.' He shared the opinion with many more that the German bombers had followed the blue flashes of electrical discharge made by the trams over head cables. It is very doubtful that this would be visible to the pilots at an altitude of 10,000 ft. favoured by the Luftwaffe for nigh time bombing,

Four of our five neighbours, who shared the common right of way over our back yards, had reason to be aware of the threat of probable bombing, as in the previous April the Borough Council with government backing had requisitioned their gardens to built a communal air raid shelter that was supposed to protect up to fifty people living in the same area. This edifice, built with red brick walls and concrete roof, reposed in the centre of a wasteland, which had previously been their gardens. This barren surreal landscape even had the original garden paths left in tact, for neighbours to traverse their way to the now isolated lavatories. There was now no privacy in the privy.

It must have been decided by officialdom that the communal shelter better suited the locale. The narrow back gardens of Devonshire Street not able to accommodate the more usual small corrugated steel Anderson shelters that held six persons. In the event, everyone took an instant dislike to this damp and gloomy monstrosity, choosing to use their own cellars for air raid protection. It would have been interesting to witness the chaos of some fifty persons stampeding down a funnel, which was our jennel, at the sound of the first air raid siren warning.

Of course, this waste land provided an ideal play ground for the kids of Devo, literally on their doorstep, and was to become the main meeting place for the start of all our gang forays. Looking back, it now amazes me that the occupants of the yard never ever raised objection, when hordes of kids descended on their property, with all the boisterousness of their youth. Edith Kennel, a resident, often had to sit on her lavatory with only the thickness of the wooden door separating her from the game of cricket taking place in the yard. The chalked wicket was displayed on the outside of her lavatory door.

There were six households in the yard. I shall describe them as I first remember them, but it was then, pretty much contemporary to late 1940.

The top two houses had their gardens and boundary fences still intact. The cobbled area, serving a right of way, was gated. The other four houses shared common waste ground at top of which were a row of lavatories forming, with a short wall, the rear boundary. The other brick built boundary wall ran along the right side adjoining the bottom house. This wall was only four feet high on the yard side, but had a drop of some eight feet on the other side, which was a builder's yard.

The top house was occupied by an elderly widow Mrs Hall at that time living alone, but would have her son Joe and daughter-in-law Dolly move in before the war ended. She was a keen gardener which was kept spick and span. Her left hand boundary was a brick built wall some six feet high, which effectively separated our yard from the one above.

Next was our house which had a large dilapidated shed in the garden close to the house.

Below us at number 18, were Len and Ethel Hubbard with Len's mother. They also had a lodger, Alice Yeomans originating from Lancashire. She again was elderly and afflicted with a club foot. Always wore a pinafore, but oddly, also wore a black apron over the piny. She also smoked dry tea leaves through a corn cob pipe. Cigarettes were scarce. There was no tea bags then, only loose tea leaves. We also, dried our spent tea leaves on our fire back for her use. She eked out a living by shopping for the locals, regularly walking to Whittington Moor, which must have been most difficult considering her walking disability. As she aged it became more difficult to carry out this service, but she kept taking orders and would solicit help from any one going 'down't moor'

I once became her unpaid errand boy when see enlisted me to get her two pounds of tomato sausage from Witham's, the premier pork butcher on Whittington Moor. The shop now trades as Watson and Brown. They still have the two pink pottery pigs on display that I used to admire back then. The package of sausages in a string bag, was hanging from my bike handlebars. As I started to ascend the slight gradient in Devonshire Street, I stood on the pedals and swung side to side to impart more pedal drive to the wheels. Yes, the string bag caught up between wheel spokes shredding the bag and spattered the sausage meat. Alice demanded and got full recompense from my Mum, who was hard up herself. The guilty feeling of costing my mum unnecessary expenditure of her hard earned money still troubles me to this day.

At number 16 was Winnie Wright, sister of her next door neighbour Ethel Hubbard. Winnie had three children, Doris a teenager, Betty, Peter and would later have Keith. Her husband Arthur, nickname 'Vultch' was serving in the 14th Army in India and then Burma. I do recall that on many evening times Winnie and her friend Kit Bond, who lived further down Devonshire Street, after a night out would be persuaded to sing a rather bawdy song that went something like this;

Now this is number one, and the fun has just begun

Roll me over, lay me down and do it again

Roll me over, in the clover

Roll me over, lay me down and do it again

Now this is number two, and I'm taking off her shoe

Roll me over, lay me down and do it again

Roll me over, in the clover

Roll me over, lay me down and do it again

Now this is number three, my hand is on her knee

Roll me over, lay me down and do it again

Roll me over, in the clover

Roll me over, lay me down and do it again

Now this is number four, she's beggin' me for more

Roll me over, lay me down and do it again

Roll me over, in the clover

Roll me over, lay me down and do it again

Now this is number five, we're startin in to jive

Roll me over, lay me down and do it again

Roll me over, in the clover

Roll me over, lay me down and do it again

Now this is number six, she's starting to do tricks

Roll me over, lay me down and do it again

Roll me over, in the clover

Roll me over, lay me down and do it again

Now this is number seven, she thinks that she's in heaven

Roll me over, lay me down and do it again

Roll me over, in the clover

Roll me over, lay me down and do it again

Now this is number eight, the doctor's at the gate

Roll me over, lay me down and do it again

Roll me over, in the clover

Roll me over, lay me down and do it again

Now this is number nine, the twins are doin fine

Roll me over, lay me down and do it again

Roll me over, in the clover

Roll me over, lay me down and do it again

Now this is number ten, we're starting it again

Roll me over, lay me down and do it again

Roll me over, Yankee soldier

Roll me over, lay me down and do it again

Arthur was demobbed in 1946 and he returned home extremely emaciated and suffered bouts of malaria, which would be the cause of his premature death.

The jennel separated the Wright's from number 14 were Roly and Edith Kennel lived with their five children Roy and Mary, both approaching adult hood, then Ethel, Anise and Brenda. A late addition would be young Roland.

Finally at the bottom of the yard lived Granny Aldred who had her extended family also living on Devonshire Street. She was secretive by nature and was regarded by us kids as a wicked witch.

Anderson shelters were issued free to poor people on less than £5 per week. My Dadad did not qualify, so he built his own personal brick and concrete family size shelter that was half buried in the back garden. Regularly used from the summer of 1940 until late autumn 1941, the shelter then gradually became less needed as the German bombing offensive in the North of England practically ceased This labyrinth would then become a secret place for us kids to frighten each other with ghost stories and play the game of truth or dare, the losers paying a forfeit of having hot melted candle wax dripped on to their bare wrists. It was also where our Esme and her friend Dorothy Coupe 'egged on' us younger kids to take a first drag of a fag end. Many stubbed out cigarettes had carelessly been left in various make shift tin lid ash trays scattered around the shelter. They smelled of damp and were soggy, but they still lit.

The house at Racecourse Road was, and still is the on one end of a block of three. The adjoining neighbours were the Shaw family. Nin's other neighbour was 'Ket' Jones whose house shared a common right of way to both properties. Ket had a large family, the middle two girls being Annie, a bit older than me, and Betty slightly younger. When I was about six, and was at my Nin's, these girls were my playmates. On one occasion there was only Annie to play with. We somehow ended up behind the air raid shelter, and began to 'explore' each others bodies. We must have known it was taboo, as I was occasionally peeping up toward the house to make sure no one was coming down the path. This action attracted the attention of Nin who discovered our compromise. To my acute embarrassment our misdemeanour got past around the family, and for years afterwards when arriving at Nin's, I would be greeted by 'Here comes Annie behind air raid shelter.'

As in common with our neighbours my parents had adapted the smaller of our cellars with the basics to provide a modicum of comfort in the event that we had to use it during an air raid. The walls had been freshly whitewashed and fitted out with home made wooden bunk beds. It was furnished with a small table and stool. A primus stove, hurricane paraffin lamp, matches, candles and torch were stored in a waxed cardboard box, there being no electric light supply.

Air raid warnings had been sounded from mid summer onwards but all had been proven false. Never the less Mum had always heeded the warnings and each occasion my brother and me had been disturbed from sleep and in a drowse state taken to the safety of the cellar. There we stayed till morning so as not to be disturbed a second time during the same night.

On the Thursday night of the first heavy bombing of Sheffield Dad had just finished work at 6.30pm and was his habit, having a couple of pints of bitter in the Victoria Inn on Shaw Street before going home. When the first siren sounded the warning of a possible air raid he took no notice thinking it was another false alarm, as he also did with second siren, warning of an immanent air raid. Even when the bombing started he was slow to react. He later told me 'At first when the bombs started to drop I didn't take it in.' Then as soon has he realised the enormity of the situation he thought: 'What about Hilda and the kids.' Even so his immediate reaction was to send his boyhood friend, Bill Titlow, (locally known as Donk and his real name was actually Bill Madin) up to Devonshire Street to keep the family company while he finished his drinking session.

Donk was a regular and familiar visitor to Devonshire Street so with no hesitation he came straight on down the cellar. Mum said when the first incendiaries lit up the night sky she ran out into the street and asked a local resident Jimuk Mellor's if he would help her carry me and our Bern down to the cellar. Jimuk's classic reply was; 'It's every man for himself tonight.' And disappeared up the street. Mum somehow managed to get us both down the cellar were Donk found the three of us safe and sound. He stayed with us until the all clear sounded, and on every other future occasion when we took shelter in that cellar Donk would be there, his presence, in his overlarge black overcoat and big cloth cap imparting to Mum and us, a calm reassurance. On such nights he kept us entertained to cause distraction from the reality, Donk would make us kids and him a hot mug of oxo, which must have taken forever on the old primus stove. He would soak bread pobs in our brew then pretend to spoon feed us the hot mush, only to withdraw it, blow on it to make it cool, then eventual feed it to us. He had always got a new playing card or coin trick to baffle our young minds with.

Bill Titlow's shrunken appearance inside his over sized attire was a result of his current medical problems. He had an acute asthmatic condition and was in advanced state of Parkinson's disease, which was manifest by the uncontrollable shake of his right arm. This disease would be the cause of his premature death.

One Sunday lunchtime as we sat around the table Dad in a rare moment talked to me and our Bern about his childhood and I recall one particular incident were Dad and Donk had been caught stealing apples from a large house on Avenue Road that was later purchased by the local bookmaker, Danny Troth.

A neighbour who had seen two boys stealing apples recognised one as Donk and reported this to the house owner who informed the local constabulary on Whittington Moor. When traced, Donk denied the incident and said he had been with his pal Walt Ellis bird nesting. Dad was then brought to the police station to corroborate Donk's statement which he immediately did. The police constable then turned to Donk and asked him where they had been bird nesting. Donk's reply was; 'Up Icky Picky Lane.' Dad said I knew then we were sunk. Apparently they were given twelve months probation which now seems to me to be a rather harsh sentence for the 'crime' of scrumping a few apples.

It is difficult for me to reach back all those years ago to explore and understand the mind set of residents of the West End during that period. I of course was there, but not able to fully comprehend these events. I have to rely on reminiscences of my family and acquaintances from that neighbourhood. There was a feeling of remoteness, brought about by their parochial lifestyle. They lived in an enclave of fortress mentality. Concerns were of immediate locality. Yes, Sheffield had been bombed, but for god sake, it was twelve miles away. This would not be allowed to upset their daily routine, and many people would choose to stay in bed, ignoring the air raid warnings. Our special constable, Bobby Hardy, no relation to us, in his self appointed post of local ARP warden could never muster a full compliment of six persons for fire watch duties; they were either in the pub or in bed.

Many residents of Devonshire Street, my dad included, when disturbed from sleep by the insistent tapping on their bedroom window by Bobby Hardy using a cloths prop, would open the window and shout! 'Bugger off you silly old fool.' 'Yes, more than a passing resemblance to Dads Army.'

In a way this isolationist mentality was proven to have some substance as after the Sheffield Blitz there were very few local incursions from German raiders. The only other significant event occurred in 1941 when a solitary German raider tried to bomb the Chesterfield Tube Company, an armaments factory

tory situated on Derby Road. The bomb missed the factory but destroyed a chip shop on the adjacent Redvers Buller Road. This upset the factories day shift as the shop had been the sole supplier of mid day chip butties.

Again, I am fully aware of Liverpudlian Stan Boardman's catch phrase.

The nearest exposure of my family to the German attacks was in early 1941 when a damaged, and lost, aircraft crash landed in a farmer's field at Barlow village. Our Sid drove all of the family up to the crash site. According to mum there was dozens of people milling about the aircraft, so she left me at the entrance gate in the arms of the local village bobby. 'It's what they call a Junkers 88 flying pencil.' The policeman told her.

This must have stuck in her mind, as for the duration of the war, when ever she wanted me and Bernard to go to bed; she would shout! 'Come on you two, up Junkers 88.' Meaning of course, go up the stairs to bed. There seems to be some confusion about the identity of this aircraft. From the description it was more likely to be a Dornier Do17 as Mum later explained: 'It had a funny tail with two big swastikas.' Research on this question has produced no information.

The end of the year of 1940 was a time for measured confidence as we had survived all that the might of Germany could throw at us. Dadad invited the Lister and Hardy extended families to join in a New Years Eve celebratory party at Racecourse Road. We younger children had earlier in the evening enjoyed our own party of Tizer, fairy cakes and a sing song in front of the Christmas tree, before being tucked comfortably into the shelters bunk beds. There was still a chance of a sudden air raid occurring. As we set off for Devonshire Street in the early morning of New Years Day I remember distinctly that I would not get in that pram being insistent that I should walk all the way back home towing behind me my week old Christmas present, a toy pull along wooden railway engine.

Chapter 3 – Pre-School

We'll talk of sunshine and of song,

And summer days, when we were young;

Sweet childish days, that where as long

As twenty days, are now

WILLIAM WORDSWORTH

Dadad, Nin and Esme Blackpool 1948

During 1941 and up to Easter 1942 prior to my commencing nursery school my week days were divided between spending the mornings at my Nin's and the afternoons with my Mum down at Dadad's yard. At Nin's I was very much left to my own devices, but generally hindered Nin whilst trying to help her prepare Dadad's dinner. I looked forward to the daily milk delivery by standing at Nin's front garden gate with a white enamel jug. The milk was delivered direct from Bowlers farm by horse and cart and poured into the jug using a pint size ladle straight from a galvanised milk churn. Delivery of coal was also by horse and cart. The ton weight of coal was unloaded by the roadside and I would then help Noah, a local character wheel barrow it to Nin's coal house. For my pains I would be spitting up coal dust for hours afterward. Noah made a living out of storing coal, he charged Nin one shilling. As a sideline he would also shovel up the horse droppings and store it in a sack he always carried with him. When the bag was full he would sell it for use as garden manure.

Sometimes Nin would let me sort out her rummage drawer in which she kept all sorts of bits and bobs, that one day might come in useful. 'Maybe you have such a drawer? I know we have.' My favourite pastime was to sit at my Dadad's bureau and play office. I would pretend to use the telephone, sort out the mail, and count out the cash. There was a real telephone, an extension from the Yard, owning a telephone then was a rarity. The cash was bundles of cancelled cheques returned from the Westminster Bank. With a white oval shaped embossed logo and beautiful scrolled violet colouring they had the appearance of real bank notes, to me, as a young child. During this period I was thought fit enough to dispense with the plaster bandages, but Mum still put me in the pram for longer journeys as I was still unsteady and took time walking. Mum always walked so fast that it was impossible for me to keep up with her. Our Bern always had to have hold of her hand and trot beside the pram to keep pace. I started to accompany Nin on her weekly Friday visit to the bank on Whittington Moor. The bank was next door to Dan Newton's Printers and Stationers shop. Whilst

Whilst my Nin when into the bank I would browse Dan Newton's window and particularly gaze at a bottle of Swan red ink, priced sixpence. How many times have I stood there, and longed to obtain that bottle of ink. When Nin emerged from the bank she would regularly say to me 'I won't be long, I have to pay some bills.' Then disappear into the next building which had a green tile facade. It would be many years before I discovered that the green tiled building was in fact the Colin Campbell public house. My Nin was always partial to a tot of Bells Scotch Whisky.

Dadad Blackpool 1948

Afternoons at the Yard were always adventurous. The yard was piled high with scrap cars which I could explore. I used to save the coloured enamel name plates which I had to prise off the car bonnets with a screw driver. My Dadad gave me a small tool kit so I could tinker with car engines that were going to be sold as heavy scrap. No there was no danger; it needed a crane to move them. Mum dealt mainly with car bodywork which she would cut into pieces using an acetylene torch. There was such a wonderful smell when she carried out this task. The bits of car bodies would be sold as light scrap. Our Sid would take me with him on most journey's and always when weighing in scrap. The weigh bridge was on Whittington Moor opposite the end of Pottery Lane. We would make the first journey with an empty truck to ascertain its weight, getting a recorded docket. The second journey was with a load of either light or heavy scrap which again was recorded. It was then off to sell it to Jack Thorpe a scrap merchant down Pottery Lane. There were some runners, cars who had still retained their wheels. Sid would sit me in such a vehicle and tow it up a slight slope using the breakdown truck's winch. When it was released I steered it back down the track. It was an exhilarating experience as I felt that I was really driving the vehicle. Dadad's office was a converted thirty foot long Victorian wood panelled railway coach, in the rear of which was an oak roll top desk and swivel chair. The desk had dozens of small compartmental drawers, some of which were not obvious, being secret. These particular drawers were assigned for my sole use and I delighted in using them to store my treasures collected in the yard.

Mum would take me and our Bern with her up to Nin's in the early evening where she would then busy herself with her cleaning chores. Nin as usual would be holding court in her kitchen with Ket Jones and an assortment of drop in acquaintances so we kids would amuse ourselves in the large living room. Our Joan, a striking looking girl who resembled my Mum was in her teenage years and working full time at Shentalls Grocers and Provision Merchants would either be reading her copy of The Red Letter (a story paper for young women) or be stuck in front of the wall mirror trying out different make up or re-styling her hair. She would also try to persuade me to let her cut my long finger nails by offering me a bribe of sixpence. My finger ends were very sensitive to touch so she never ever succeeded with this ploy. Esme would usually have her friend Marina Bagguly for company and Bern and I would sit around the large dining table with them playing card games such as Fish, Rummy and Pontoon. Getting a little more boisterous all four of us on hands and knees would follow each other around the floor and end up under the table, the underside of which was littered with patches of age hardened chewing gum, as testament to past children's play. Even at my early age this particular game heightened my sensual awareness of being in intimate contact with the girls that stirred in me unexplainable feelings of excitement ignited further by sight of their navy blue knickers in my face, and the whiff of their sensuous body odour.

My time at home during weekends and holidays were usually spent in the back yard that had once been four separate gardens, now an area of waste ground where the neighbourhood kids would congregate to play. Just below the compacted ash surface layer there was to be found hundreds of bits of broken crocks, many having intricate colour patterns mainly of blue and white. The finest ones called 'Pot money' were in demand and often traded for fag cards (cigarette cards) and popties (glass marbles). There was a disused pottery at the top of Devonshire Street so maybe the houses had been built on its rubbish tip. A sea shell was once found and we took turn in holding it up to our ear to listen to the sound of the sea. It sounded clearer facing the bottom wall so we thought that was the direction to Skegness. Unfortunately that direction was north. We boys played marbles, football and cricket. The girls were always skipping in time to the tune the big ship sails on the alley-alley- ho and;

Doctor Foster went to Gloucester

In a shower of rain

He fell in a puddle

Right up to his Middle

An never was seen again

Together we would play Hop-scotch by scratching out the play area in the dust and use a piece of crock as a marker. We also would run around with a yard brush between our legs and slapping our thighs pretending to cowboys and cowgirls. Roger Huckerby had a large iron band from off a wooden beer barrel that his Uncle Sherwood managed to get him. We would take it in turns to bowel the hoop around a marked out oval track using a stick to drive it along. The winner was the one who could complete the most laps without touching the line.

If we were in the back fields we may spend an entire afternoon down at the thistle patch catching Bumble bees in a glass jar. Or if just lazing in the sunshine, the girls would make Daisy chains and thread them through their hair or simply pull the petals off a daisy; he loves me, he loves me not! The boys would pluck a Celandine or Buttercup and hold it under a girls chin; if it tickled she liked butter, or blowing on a dandelion 'clock' to tell time. We would all just lie in the field chewing on a new green grass shoot, how sweet they were. Or maybe search for a four leaf clover in the hundreds of red and white flowered clover patches. The newly mown haystacks in Mason's fields were perfect for diving through although you itched for days afterwards.

In September of 1941 Mum had taken me and our Bern to Stephenson's Arcade to visit their toy department Christmas display. There I saw a magnificent papier-mâché model castle complete with operating drawbridge. It was priced at £2.10s.0d which was nearly as much as Dad earned in a week. I had set my heart on it but realised that Mum and Dad could not possibly afford it and was resigned to that fact. As Christmas Eve came round I still harboured dreams of Santa bringing me that special gift and with fingers crossed I closed my eyes very tight in hope of going off to sleep so as not to disturb him, for had not Lilly Umney who was baby sitting told me and our Bern that Mum had left her with two bottles of pale ale and two mince pies to bribe him with? I looked under my side the bed on Christmas morning and as expected there was nothing. I completely circled the bed and there was still nothing except the stocking that I had expectantly hung over the bottom bed post. Surly my 'Fort' could not fit inside this? No it couldn't, for on inspection it contained a toffee apple and a net bag of chocolate coins covered with gold foil. I woke up our Bern and asked him he could find my fort. He looked under his side of the bed and came up grinning all over his face as he showed me the 'case ball' that he so desperately wanted. "Sorry kid, looks like Santa didn't see thee" he said. Utterly devastated I went into Mum and Dads bedroom and found them fast asleep. I shook Mum. "Santa's not been." Dad replied "We saw him last night he was too drunk to get upstairs, go and see if he's still downstairs." I tiptoed down stairs and peeped into the kitchen, he was not there. I crept across to the middle door and gingerly open it, and there on the dining table was my Fort. All those previous weeks Mum had scrimped enough money to meet the weekly payments for my fort and our Bern's leather football. I truly loved that fort and it gave me great pleasure for many, many years. I was really grateful and appreciative of the sacrifices Mum made then for us two, and would continue to do so all her life. God bless her.

Due to the blackout condition prevailing throughout the war years of the main entertainment most evenings, especially in autumn and winter months, was the radio or wireless as we called it.

There was something almost desperately reassuring by the BBC's programming, an attempt, perhaps, to convince people all was well and the war was just a mild irritant.

There was light music; typical were *Workers Playtime, The Henry Hall Orchestra* light comedy with *Hi Gang* with Ben Lyon, Bebe Daniels and Vic Oliver, *Band Wagon* with Arthur Askey the satirical comedy *ITMA* It's that man again, with Tommy Handley working at the Ministry of Disinformation The most scaring program for me as young child was the Wednesday broadcast of *The Man In Black*, later as *Appointment with Fear* narrated by Valentine Dyall, who in an affected sinister voice told macabre tales of mystery and the supernatural. I remember one evening listening with suspense to a tale of two friends, one of whose sister had been the victim of a human vampire. They had just discovered the daytime resting place of this vampire and were about to drive a wooden stake through his heart, when there was a knock on our door. Being Wednesday it could only be our insurance man, Mr Thompson, calling for his weekly four penny premium. As usual Mum did not have the money, and as usual we would turn the wireless volume down and hide behind the settee. Mr Thompson was nothing if not persistent as he would peep through the letter box, then try to peep under the blackout sheet, and then knock again, then go through the jennel and try the back door. He knew we were at home but eventually he gave up realising that he would go empty handed yet again. This fiasco usually lasted a good ten minutes and on this particular night I never did hear if the two friends had actually destroyed the vampire.

Children's Hour a radio programme devised for younger listeners was always transmitted on the BBC Home Service at five o'clock. An early favourite programme was *Toytown* concerning the adventures and escapades of Larry the Lamb and his influential friend Dennis the Daschund. Larry the innocent dupe always fell foul of the inhabitants of Toytown chiefly Mr Grouser, Ernest the Policeman, and the Mayor, usually on the road to Arkville. Larry the Lamb with his distinctive tremulous voice was played by Derek McCullock, 'Uncle Mac', who went on to be in charge of programmes, and later to present a children's song request program, *Children's Favourites*, with the most requested song being *The Laughing Policeman*. Uncle Mac always closed Children's Hour acting as a surrogate parent to the thousands of evacuee children so far from home with 'Goodnight children, everywhere.'

Later programmes that influenced me were *Romany, with his dog Raq*. Romany, who was of gypsy descent, gave talks on the countryside. Also to my mind a more evocative program *Wandering with Nomad*, another nature program, were, Nomad accompanied by a young boy, would describe to him the flora and fauna as they walked through a particular area of countryside. How I wished that I was that boy. My all time favourite was *Jennings at School* the hilariously reckless misdoings of a boarding school boy Jennings to the consternation of his friend Darbishire. In one episode Jennings for a bet, deliberately got his head stuck between two iron railings and had Darbishire call the fire brigade. This reminds me of the time that we as a family had been to the first house at the Lyceum cinema on Whittington Moor and then went into the beer garden of the Red Lion just opposite the cinema. Dad bought each of us, me and our Bern, a small bottle of soft drink. Of course, as was his bent, Bernard guzzled his drink down and then stuck his index finger into the neck of the bottle. Try as everyone might, his finger would not come free of the bottle. He had walk home with the bottle intact, and has last resort Dad had to use a hammer to break the bottle neck. Our Bern inherited his Mums looks having the angelic features of an angel but this belied the devilish impudence that was characteristic of his nature.

The tunes again reflected the mood with *When They Sound the Last All-Clear, The White Cliffs of Dover* and *Lili Marlene* the latter being popular with both the German and Allied troops then fighting in North Africa. I have an original 78 rpm recoding by Lale Anderson of Lili Marlene which I treasure. The film industry at this time produces many, many, what are now recognised as classic films dominated by *Casablanca*. This quintessential 40s film is still remembered for piano-playing Dooley Wilson's singing of *As Time Goes By* and Bogies (Humphrey Bogart) memorable line 'Here's looking at you, kid.' Other classic were Richard Llewellyn's novel adaptation of *How Green was my Valley* and *Mrs Miniver* starring Greer Garson. For the younger cinema goer there were Walt Disney's full length animation of *Dumbo* and *Bambi*.

Visiting the cinema was second only in entertainment popularity after listening to the radio in our case the first house at six o'clock at the Lyceum on Saturday evenings. We would normally be back home by eight thirty. Prior to the visit it was tin bath time in the kitchen for me, Bernard and Esme, my mother's youngest sister who was two years older than Bernard. Nin had a bathroom with modern plumbing with the luxury of hot water on tap, but Esme loved to 'rough it' at Devonshire Street. The bath water was drawn from the copper which had been fired up during the afternoon and was topped up with hot water from a kettle after each bath. Esme was always last out of the bath and by that time, the towel, which was full of holes was also soaking wet, which meant Mum had to virtually pat her dry, and if we had a fire lit, she would stand in front of it to finish the drying process. We three Esme, Bernard, and me in the pram, would set off to the Lyceum in advance of Mum and Dad, as they had still to get ready, and as there was always a queue forming, we would save their place in it. On one particular evening, in early 1942, we set off as normal with me in the pram, Esme pushing, and Bernard holding on to the pram side. We had reached the bottom of Scarsdale Road and was about to cross over the main Sheffield road which was just a few minutes away from the Lyceum when Esme decided that she would now ride in the pram. With Esme now in the pram and Bernard pushing they started across the road with me toddling behind. I woke up in the Chesterfield Royal Hospital some six hours later having been knocked down by a car. I had suffered concussion and sustained a fractured right arm and bruised ribs. It must also have caused a shock for the driver, a lady, who according to witnesses had no chance of avoiding hitting me. She personally delivered me to the Casualty Department of the hospital and stayed with me until Mum and Dad arrived. I was discharged after three days and I was never again to use that, or any other pram.

Chapter 4 – Infant School

All that we know who lie in gaol

Is that the wall is strong;

And that each day is like a year

A year whose days are long.

OSCAR WILDE

The Ballad of Reading Gaol

'You'll be goin to school after Easter' Mum told me. She explained: 'Since I've to work down't Yard they've let you start a bit early. Weren't that good of um?' Mum phrased the question in such a way as to give me no option but to nod my head in agreement. I definitely did not want to go to school as I was content with going up to Nin's and down to the Yard. Nothing could be more exciting than this. Another thing, I couldn't leave poor Nin in the lurch because she told me 'It'll be a weight of my mind when tha goes to school.' I knew she didn't mean it cos she kept telling me 'I'll never get shut o thee.'

The fabric that was Edmund Street School some seventy decades ago is still identifiable to this day as the Cavendish Junior School. Back then, the school also had nursery entry level accommodated in a prefabricated single story building situated on the opposite side of the road. On first acquaintance with this newly purpose built nursery unit, in April of 1942, I was at once eager to be rid of my nervously fussy Mum, and immerse myself in this children's colourful and exciting wonderland of wooden building bricks, large seesaws, climbing frames, a huge sandpit and all manner of brick-a-brac all smelling like one of my new toy soldiers. There was a big table where kids were painting and gluing and using scissors. And most inviting in the special rest room I was shown my very own little bed, a blue painted wooden frame enclosing a gaily patterned mattress that I would use during the class afternoon nap. All too soon this introductory morning session was over and I couldn't wait for Monday morning to come round to begin my new life at school.

I certainly looked forward to starting at Nursery School and I was not to be disappointed as I was welcomed by a kindly lady who showed me where to hang my coat, pointed out the toilet and where I should wash my hands. I cannot remember her name or any of the three other ladies there only that they all wore dark blue uniforms resembling nurses. On leaving the cloakroom we entered the large open plan classroom where all the kids were sat cross legged in front of a lady playing a piano and were singing away to their hearts content. I may be wrong but I believe they were singing *All Things Bright and Beautiful*. The tune was familiar but I did not know the words very well. I was invited to sit down and the kids made room for me and I just mumbled the word, but I didn't care, I was just as content as I could be.

The nursery unit was less like a school and more like a crèche as the ethos was 'learning through play.' It was equipped with stimulating educational toys and games and a range of larger and smaller equipment to encourage physical development. We experienced a simple structure for the day with a wide variety of early learning activities planned to develop and extend our skills and enable us to gain confidence. We learned letter and number recognition and counting skills using lovely pearl cowrie shells. The ones standing for ten had a black dot marked on them. We had to wash our hands regularly, especially after going to the toilet. This was called hygiene awareness. I do remember that many a time I would arrive home with chapped hands. Music with the piano was central to learning and bonding from morning assembly to group singing nursery rhymes and marching around the classroom. The unit had a large wooden Noah's Ark complete with brightly painted cut out wooden figures and animals. This was used for telling stories, animal recognition and appreciation of the big world. I became completely absorbed when the ark was used and was delighted when able to touch and feel the tactile figures. I often wished that I could take it home with me and lo and behold as if preordained one Saturday whilst shopping with Mum on Whittington Moor I espied an Ark in the window of West's Newsagents. It wasn't as big and impressive as ours at school but this Walt Disney cardboard model with all the Disney characters was to me more desirable. It cost nine pence; a lot of money, but to my surprise Mum said I could have it. I took the completed cut out model to school the next Monday and was delighted that it was admired and displayed along side the big ark.

To offset the meagre diets due to wartime shortages and rationing and promote a healthy community of children the government supplied supplements of free milk, cod-liver oil and concentrated orange to all primary school children. We would line up at morning break and be given a third of a pint bottle of milk and straw then had ten minutes in which to drink it down. At dinner time we would sit on our teeny chairs in groups of six around a circular table and when finished and just before our afternoon nap be given a spoonful of evil smelling cod-liver oil that made you gag. We were told it was to keep out the cold so we obediently swallowed it down. The concentrated orange juice was obtained by Mum from the Children's Health Clinic just across the road from the nursery. She used to give me and Bern a spoonful every day. The afternoon nap was something I always looked forward to. At home I would always have a couple of hours sleep on Mums bed in the afternoon. I was a very heavy sleeper and one particular afternoon I woke up and asked Mum where my 'Green Train' was? Mum had no idea what I was talking about, but I was persistent that I had a green train. I had been sleeping so heavily that the dream took on realism. At nursery I would snuggle down in my little bed and immediately drop off in a deep sleep. 'What could be more wonderful than this?' Well I was told that going up to the big school across the road would be more adventurous. Sadly for me this would not be the case.

On the first morning at Edmund Street Infants School all the new starters were confronted in the playground by Miss Harding, the Headmistress. The very sight of her filled me with dread. She was even more frightening than our Bern had said. I recall a classroom scene in Dennis Potter's *The Singing Detective* were the young Philip Marlowe is terror stricken by a tyrannical teacher. Miss Harding was a dead ringer in appearance of the portrayed teacher except Miss Harding also wore rimless glasses that gave an even more cruelly merciless spectral image. When Miss Harding rang the bell for attention her spoken manner was of distain, for many of the children standing in the playground that morning were ragged arsed with cardboard covering the holes in their shoes being undernourished, and suffered from all manner of minor skin ailments such as boils, the most noticeable being scabies, as the sufferer was usually shaven headed, and covered in patches of gentian violet, which stained the skin and scalp with purple colouring. After sending the regular attendees to morning assembly Miss Harding, now accompanied by four teachers, began a role call of pupils to be assigned to each class teacher. I stood there petrified as each name was called hoping against hope that when she eventually called my name she would not recognise it. There appeared to be no hint of recognition in the matter of fact manner in which she assigned me to Mrs Beasley's class.

I do recall on entering the classroom of the overwhelming smell of wax and disinfectant and the Victorian austerity of bare high walls of brickwork, gloss painted custard cream over dark green, on which were secured wrought iron window ventilator mechanisms, operated by worm screw actuating handles and large central heating radiators whose pipe work ran all around the room. There was little in way of decoration other than a religious picture and a large colour chart of a map of the world. My single seat oak desk had seen better days having deep scour marks mostly in filled with blue ink. The desk had a white pottery inkwell with marked evidence of containing vivid blue ink and a writing pen that reposed in a groove. The desk top would open but on inspection revealed nothing inside. Mrs Beasley proved to be an excellent teacher and a kindly person who always appeared to be genuinely interested in my development and welfare. On one occasion I had drawn a picture of a frog during an art lesson. It must have had some merit as Mrs Beasley requested that I show it to the other classes. I was so intimidated by the Headmistress, and fearing that I may walk in on one of her classes, I hid in the boy's lavatory for a time before returning to my class, trusting Mrs Beasley would not further mention it in the staffroom.

Miss Harding regularly patrolled the school yard at dinner time, her eagle eye missing nothing. My brother Bernard, who attended the same school, was two years ahead of me. He fell foul of Miss Harding's vigilance, as she caught him at the rear of the toilet block kissing a class mate, Joan Hallows. After caning him she took him back to Miss Sherwood's classroom, paraded him in front his entire classmates to public shame him. She then made him deliver a letter to Mum I was not told the content of this letter but I remember Mum going ballistic at our Bernard. As a child, Bernard sometimes acted rashly, before thinking of consequence. In his class Joan Hallows sat in front of our Bernard. A few days after the caning Joan began to gloat to him how she had not been punished for the kissing incident. In retaliation he loaded a pen from his ink well and spattered Joan's fair haired plaits with the vivid blue ink... Miss Sherwood had to report this demeanour to the Headmistress, with the result of a second caning in front of the whole school assemblage. Miss Harding insisted that Mum and Dad personally apologise to Joan's parents. They also had to meet the cost to have the ink stain clipped out of Joan's hair. This was the first and only time that Dad thrashed either of us. I do not argue with Miss Harding's authority in this matter, but I do question the severity and manner of punishment of such a young child.

I started at the big school being rather shy but with the intention to work hard and enjoy what was on offer and being fully aware of the misdemeanours of my big brother I was determined to keep out of trouble and try my best to keep out of the way of Miss Harding if at all possible. Unfortunately all my good intentions came to naught through a rather silly fracas. One playtime I was playing a game of Spitfires with a group of kids who were chasing me, the Messerschmitt, all of us with arms outspread and tearing around the playground. Being still rather unsteady on my legs I accidentally stumbled into a class mate Alan Freeman from Sheepbridge Crescent. Alan was a popular kid who got on with everybody. Just as I was saying sorry, Peter Cooper a kid I didn't know from Adam, butted in and said 'Ellis just cos tha comes from West End tha thinks tha tough.' with that he punched me in the face which gave me a nose bleed. The incident somehow got to the ears of Miss Harding who caned both of us. My finger ends were still numb with pain when I got home from school at dinner time but I said nowt to Mum.

The ultimate betrayal at Edmund Street was when I was in Miss Lindsey's class. Miss Harding entered the classroom accompanied by a cheerful looking young lady and told me that I should go with this young lady across to the clinic. The smiling lady said something to the effect: 'Come along my brave soldier' whilst taking my hand. At the clinic I had five teeth removed and then sent back to my classroom by myself. Yes, this did happen, and yes, I was traumatised. After this incident I can recall very little more of my time at Edmund Street, only that for the most part, it was bleak. I do remember that Mrs Beasley and Miss Lindsey were imaginative and sympathetic teachers who must have taught me the core skills of reading, writing and simple arithmetic and also to be expressive in other media for I had acquired quite proficient skills in such areas when going up to junior education at Gilbert Heathcoat School.

It was really in 'out of school hours' that my mind is full of memories from that time;

It was the case that the children, some not yet five, were allowed to go home at dinner time on their own, and return in the same manner. 'How times have changed.'

These unsupervised periods did present opportunity to truant from the afternoon sessions to partake in more interesting activities as I increasingly did. On one occasion Keith Tasker, his older sister Avril, and myself, whilst absenting from school on a sunny afternoon engaged ourselves in catching Bumble Bees with a jam jar and piece of cardboard, from around a thistle patch at the bottom of the field behind our house. On several occasions I spent afternoons on my own in the back fields reproducing copies of a toy soldier. I would melt bits of old lead pipe in a tin can over a fire then pour this into an impression of the soldier made in the heavy clay soil. This method only produced what was in the clay impression leaving a flat surface where the lead puddle levelled off, so I ended up having what you might call 'half an army.' I remember pondering how on earth they manage to achieve the whole figure.

These fleeting interludes of blissful contentment always provoked repercussion, as on the following days the council appointed Attendance Officer, Walter 'Bobby' Woods, after visiting Edmund Street School to get names and addresses of children who had not attended, would in due course, come cycling up Devonshire Street and stop at number twenty, seeking an explanation of the reason for the absenteeism, from a nonplus parent. Whom one hoped, was not at home.

Ridding brook came within fifty yards distant of a point were Edmund Street met with Racecourse Road. At this point the brook was straddled by a footbridge that provided access to a bridle path, crossing two meadows belonging to Duston Farm. The course of the brook as far down as the Yard was bordered by allotments and stank of rotten cabbage and green blanket weed. After school finished for the day a favourite pastime for class mates, me included, was to go down to the brook bottom just upstream of the footbridge and race model boats made out of half of a wooden cloths peg with a paper sail. After they were launched there was a scamper onto the footbridge, to witness them re-appear on the downstream side. The boats were then followed down the brook until they disappeared into a culvert under Dunston Road close by the Yard. It always makes me smile when I hear the twaddle spouted about A.A.Milne inventing the game of pooh sticks, the racing of sticks in a stream, as told in the story of Winnie the Pooh. This enjoyable activity comes as natural to young children as does skimming stones across a stretch of water.

That tree pipit egg was the start of a passion for collecting bird eggs that lasted for many years for my brother and me. We never removed more that one egg from a clutch and never collected duplicates. It was not illegal then, as it is today, to collect wild bird eggs. In fact it was a popular hobby and collectors came from every background including medical practitioners and the clergy. I would regularly go nesting up the brook bottom after school at Edmund Street, sometimes with friends but mostly on my own. On one occasion I had been watching a Hedge Sparrows nest from its inception of building. I had already got an egg of this species so was watching its progress out of pure interest. I did not have to disturb the nest as the bush it was in was set low on the river bank and had easy access to view. The hen was laying an egg a day but on the third day there were three small blue green eggs and one slightly larger and light grey brown in colour. This puzzled me so I went to consult Jim Booth, a man older than my father, and a keen amateur naturalist who lived at the bottom of Devonshire Street. Of course I should have known it was a cuckoo's egg. This was added to our collection. The Hedge Sparrow was colloquially called a 'Dickey' by kids from the West End and I recall a rather amusing incident relating to this name on an occasion whilst nesting. I would be ten or eleven years old at the time, as a group we kids were walking alongside a hedge row when young Alan Pashley, who would be about five years old pointed to the hedge bottom and shouted 'look a dickey's with six in' It was in fact a Pheasant's nest containing over a dozen kaki coloured eggs nearly the size of hens eggs.

It was Jim Booth who later gave me a magazine called the Egg Collector, in which there was an advertisement from C.H.Gowland an ornithologist and dealer in wild bird eggs living on the Wirral Peninsula Liverpool. We duly corresponded with C.H.Gowland and received from him/her numerous price lists, including one offering specialist hermetically sealed mahogany chests of drawers suitable for butterfly or egg collectors priced from £80.00. This was when the average weekly wage for an unskilled man was less that £4.00 per week. However, C.H.Gowland did, for a number of years, supply us with eggs, mostly sea birds such as Puffin, Guillemot, Gannet, Razorbill, Gulls and Terns, for very little cost. The careful packaging ensured that we never, ever received damaged eggs. Many years later Ray Towers, a work colleague at Rolls-Royce Ltd., who was also a school governor, presented on our behalf this catalogued collection to the Science Department of the Mortimer Wilson School at Alfreton.

Chapter 5 – Lilly Umney

If you have knowledge,

Let others light their candles in it.

MARGARET FULLER

Between five and six years old I had a regular baby sitter on two evenings a week when Mum was not working at Nins. Dad on week days would normally arrive home from work at about 7.00pm. After having a strip wash at the kitchen sink he would have his tea, listen to the latest news on the radio then set out for the Railway Hotel Public House by 8.00pm. Two days a week Mum, at 8.30pm, would follow Dad down to the Pub. They would return at 10.15pm. The baby sitter was a neighbour's daughter Lilly Umney who would be aged about eighteen years old. She was a kind, sweet and gentle soul who would in the course of twelve months teach me many things in the hour period before she put me to bed. Lilly was also be supposed to baby sit our Bern, but as soon as Mum had cleared the bottom of the street he was off out. Lilly taught me lots about paper crafts and how to make paste from flour and water. We made a kite using cane sticks string and newspaper. It had long tailings made from rags. It flew remarkably well. She taught me how to French Knit using a wooden bobbin (cotton reel) having around its centre hole four steel pins which were used to weave the wool on. The wooden bobbin was also used to make a 'wind up' tank propelled by an elastic band, matchstick, and a piece of candle tallow as a bearing. We would sit and peg a rug using Hessian sacking as the base and cut up strips of waste material pushed through with half of a sharpened wooden clothes peg. She taught me the game of Draughts and we had games until I could always best her. On reflection maybe she let me win.

Lilly also introduced, Esme, Bernard and me to Sunday school at St Chads Anglican Church on Avenue Road. It was quite pleasant to listen to the bible stories, but the main attraction was the coloured pencils and drawing paper freely available for our use. Every week we would receive a coloured attendance stamp illustrating a biblical scene. These were mounted in a beautifully presented album. Lilly was a philatelist and would purchase world postage stamps from approval sheets supplied by Freddy Jones her next door neighbour. She introduced me to Freddy, who would be then about seventeen years old, and consequently, I began collecting stamps, and still do. Freddy was also a competent draughtsman and taught me how to sketch. My favourite was a profile drawing of a German Messerschmitt Me 109 fighter aircraft. He, always pedantic, would remind me to include its radio aerial. I personally thought it ruined its streamlining.

After I turned seven years old, Lilly went into service becoming a companion to an elderly lady and I was not to see her again for more than thirty years. Her legacy lingered on as on a particular Sunday night Bern and I were left on our own whilst Mum went down to meet Dad at the pub. Bern immediately went out to join up with Ronnie Huckerby a lad of his own age and cousin of Roger. Apparently they spent the evening climbing from roof to roof down Devonshire Street. Meanwhile I busied myself in making a model of a fairground Waltzer ride out of blue sugar wrapping paper and Lilly's home made flour paste which astonished and delighted my Dad on his arrival home. It was not often that we got to talk with Dad so this was especially memorable.

That is not to say that I spent all of my spare time in the house, on the contrary, most of my time was spent out and about with the Devonshire Street lads. On dark nights and also with the blackout still in force one of our more exhilarating pastimes was to go from garden to garden 'hedge hopping', The front gardens of such places as Racecourse Road were separated by rows of privet hedges and we would dive head first over each one, consecutively, never ever thinking what may be the consequence on the other side. I cannot recall anyone coming to harm, albeit, there was superficial damage to the gardens. We also played the game 'Jack, Jack shine a light' in the back fields. Someone was nominated to be 'On', the others, each with a torch, would disperse. On the command from the nominated player 'Jack, Jack shine a light' the others would flash their torch on then off. From these signals the nominated player had to try and judge where a player might be and then tag them. This game was played through the war period and for a few years afterwards. When the back fields had just started to be developed, in the latter half of 1947 for local authority housing, we were playing the game when Pete Wright ran into stacked sheets of heavy gauge wire lattice used for re-enforcing concrete rafts. His calf at the side of the shin bone was pierced deeply by a rusty projection. We took him into our shed and poured neat dettol disinfectant over the wound then bound it with an old tie. For weeks afterwards the area around the wound was a vivid blue colour.

If we just roamed the street area we would mainly gather round the gas lamp or play prankster games like the 'bull roar,' stuffing a newspaper up a roof drain pipe and setting it alight, the resulting noise would guarantee to disturb the house occupant, and a variation where we would push a lighted newspaper under someone's front door, making sure that the occupants were alerted by shouting 'Fire!' Another 'giggle' was to thread a needle with an attached button just below it. The needle would be pushed into a window frame and the black cotton played out across the street and into a jennel. When the cotton was gently pulled the button would make a tapping noise on the window. Sometimes the inhabitant would look outside on a number of occasions and still not see the attachment. In the daytime the girls would play Hopscotch or be rotational skipping to such rhythmic tunes as;

1, 2, 3, 4, 5

Once I caught a fish alive

6, 7, 8, 9, 10

Then I let it go again

Why did I let it go?

Because it bit my finger so

Which finger did it bite?

The little finger on the right

1, 2, 3, spells out.

We would play 'Peggy'. The peggy, a small piece of wood, tapered at both ends, was placed at the end of the coursey (causeway) drain gutter. Using the gutter as a guide a stick would be used to propel the peggy forwards trying to avoid a group of kids waiting catch it. If successful, the peggy would then be tapped on one end which caused it to lift, and then hit with the stick to send it as far as possible. This procedure was repeated three times. The object of the game was to estimate how many running steps it would take to reach the peggy from the end of the drain gutter. Then set a challenge to the opposing team to meet this. If successful they won, if unsuccessful the game was repeated. Then there was 'British Bulldog' a boisterous catching game were a catcher (bulldog) would stand in a marked out area and runners would try to cross the area without being held by the bulldog for a count of one, two, three. If caught they would become another bulldog. The last standing runner was the winner. 'Realio' was a variation of Bulldog were the runner would try to tag a marker and shout 'realio' to release other captured runners of his side. 'Kick-Can' was also a chase and tag game where a player would try to seek out and catch another player at the same time try defend a base tin can from being kicked away. If the can was kicked away any caught players would be released. Another boisterous game was 'Husky Busky' were the group was divided into two teams. One team would form a kind of inline rugby scrum with the lead player's outstretched hands supported against a wall. The opposing team would then, one by one, fling themselves onto the formation, each adding their own weight in an attempt to collapse the line. If the line held then the last mounted player would shout; 'husky busky finger or thumb?' If answered correctly then the teams would interchange. If the call was incorrect then they would have to withstand another onslaught.

Harrison's Builders yard next door to Mrs Aldred was a real Pandora's Box that provided free to us kids all sorts of scrap materials that had accumulated from house renovations. Our garden shed was used as a workshop to recycle such materials; Pete Wright had got hold of a panel of plywood veneer and suggested that we could use it to make boomerangs. The first one we fret sawed out was shaped like a tradition boomerang but disappointedly, when thrown would not come back to us. We gradually refined the shape until it looked more like a horseshoe than a boomerang before it worked. You could stand in the middle of Racecourse Mount and throw it right over Billy Bunting's yard, about 50 yards, and it would return to hand every time. What a result! We would beg off-cuts of deal wood, to make sledges, trolleys, scooters and display cases for our ever increasing bird egg collection.

I myself begged a zinc and enamel hearth plate from which we fashioned out barbed arrow and spear heads using a hammer and cold chisel. Our first bows and arrows were just cuttings from willow and hazel wood and were not very effective. After seeing Errol Flynn as Robin Hood we began to fashion our bows and arrows. We would spoke shave the length of the bow at front and back to make it flatter, then re-enforce the centre with a shorter piece of willow that was secured by electrical insulation tape. The arrows were made from split deal wood, again spoke shaved with quill feather flights (obtained from Dan Newton's stationary shop) and fitted with barbed head that replaced the heavy dart tip. This new setup was able to shoot an arrow well over one hundred yards. Later the zinc arrow heads, which tended to bend on impact, would be replaced with one's fashioned out of broken mechanical hacksaw blades which were lethal.

Talking about lethal reminds me of an 'incident' that occurred one summer Sunday evening. The group of 'six' gang members were standing at the top of Devo having spent most of the day in the den. Winifred Bond a child of about five years old emerged from their jennel some three quarters of the way down the street and was heading towards Jack Slight's shop. Roger Huckerby, who persisted in keeping dart barrels on the tip of his arrows, loosed off an arrow which hit Winifred in the lower leg. Someone, maybe it was our Bern quipped 'good shot Rog.' I remember that Peter Wright and I rushed down the street to give assistance. The arrow had pierced the calf but not hit the bone. We took her back home, knowing full well that her mother Kit would be out with Winnie Wright. Pete told her eldest sister, Barbara, that it was a pure accident as the arrow was shot off before Winifred appeared on the street. Unbelievably, there was no repercussion. I will not try to defend this heinous act, only to say that all of us were guilty of such mindless acts at that time, but I know for a fact that Roger's idea was just to frighten the girl by a 'near miss,' unfortunately his 'joke' misfired.

Soon after the commencement of second blitz on London in the late summer of 1944 by the German V1 Flying Bomb or Doodlebug, and later the V2 Rocket, several families in Devonshire Street took in Evacuees, children sent from London for safety from the indiscriminate bombing. Mrs Umney, Lilly's mother, took in three girls who had arrived as part of the Gill family of six children from Edmonton, North London. The eldest girl with the two youngest boys was staying with a family on Mountcastle Street. Our family became close friends with Sheila and Audrey, two of the girls staying with Mrs Umney as they both paralleled our own ages. The elder one, Barbara, was very restless, and understandably homesick, unfortunately bringing about grief to Mrs Umney's family and causing mayhem in her class at the then overcrowded, Edmund Street Junior Girls School. The eldest girl Joyce, who was the matriarch of the family, was a calming influence to the whole family, particularly with regard to Barbara's unsettled problem. After Sheila and Audrey return to London we kept in regular correspondence with for over twenty years, well after all of us had our own families.

There was another evacuee named Jimmy Sheedy from Shoreditch staying with the Burton family at number twenty six. Jimmy was a lonely undernourished boy with a nervous disposition that caused him to stutter when speaking. He was also a persistent bed wetter, as indeed I was for a short time, to the discomfort of our Bern who had to sleep in the same bed which had a lumpy flock mattress on which I peed more than once in my earliest years; the staining, scrubbed and deodorised left a off white patch on the dark blue cover, never allowing me to forget my first serious humiliation in life for when Mum would fall out with her mother, which happened on a regular basis, I naturally took her side and on occasions that I would be waiting for, or getting off a bus outside of Nin's her and Esme would come out screaming at me 'piss bed, piss bed.' At that time I could never understand why they hated Mum so much and why I was being humiliated in this way. Jimmy was completely out of his comfort zone of the East End of London in the relative open countryside that bordered the West End. He would sit on our back wall for hours gazing at a herd of cows grazing in Mason's fields and with his stutter would keep repeating 'Moo cows I'll give you a penny if you don't eat me.' I often wonder what became of him.

Chapter 6 – Street Drama

All the worlds a stage,

And all the men and women merely players:

They have their exits and their entrances;

And one man in his time plays many parts.

WILLIAM SHAKESPEARE

As You Like It

Football team 1947 – Back row (left to right): Eric Sheppard, Gerald Hall, Barry Webster. Middle row: Keith Webster, Desmond Linney, Tommy Hardy, Bernard Ellis, Peter Smith. Front row: Peter Wright, Michael Hall (mascot), Brian Ellis, Keith Tasker.

As the year turned to 1944 I became aware that there was a culture of children's street activities that mirrored the seasons, and this rhythm had been passed down from generation to generation;

Each Saturday morning in spring time the kids of Devonshire Street would set out a stall of bric-a-brac (rescued items from the traditional spring clean) under their widow and other kids would come along and try to win a selected item, by landing on it, a skimming fag card. The unsuccessful cards were kept by the store holders. I recall that Annise Kennel lost over twenty fag cards whilst trying to win a 'cut glass' sugar sifter with a red plastic screwed cap. Annis had set her heart on giving the sifter to her mother for her birthday. She never could have won it because it was stood upright. Being 'soft as grease' I gave her the sifter and returned her cards.

Jack Slights shop on lower Mountcastle Street always stocked up with Whips and Tops in readiness for the start of the spring school term at Whitsuntide.

All the lads in Devonshire Street favoured the 'Window Breaker' top as against the more common Spinning Top. When whipped the spinning top could be made to move about three feet, whereas the widow breaker could be made to travel through the air some twenty feet... Throughout the spring we would whip the top all the way to school and also all the way back home. If you had some expertise you actually, with your top, knock a similar one out of its trajectory. If you had an evil streak like our Bern you could 'accidentally' hit a person with it.

School summer holidays signalled weeks of unfettered play – play that cost nothing. On the top of the back fields, there came together dozens of West End kids of every age group ranging from five to fifteen to participate in the activity of 'Throwing Arrows' The hand made arrows were thrown by of looping a knotted string just below the flights then taking the string down towards the point before winding it around the third and index fingers. When thrown by the bigger lads the arrows would nearly reach the brook some hundred and fifty yards distant. Thrown by us kids it might travel half that distance. We discovered that the best flights were made from playing cards, and most packs on the West End were missing the odd card or two.

This was also the time for Pea-shooters and Catapults that we called 'Flirters' If you were lucky you could beg a piece of glass tubing off Leonard Linney who was employed as a Glass Blower down at the BTH works on Whittington Moor. I normally had to settle for a section of the hollowed stalked Cow Parsley which tasted putrid but did make a very effective shooter. Being scarce we never used peas for the pellets instead we used Hawthorne berries that we colloquially called 'aigues.'

Bernard and I would supply most of the West End kids with pieces of car wheel inner tube rubber to use for their flirters. The rest of the flirter was made up from a piece of leather from an old shoe tongue and a wooden straddle cut from an apple tree. In later years as we ventured through Sheepbridge Works to meet kids from the Square we would sneak into the Forge workshops and fill our pockets with steel 'puncheons ' that made excellent, if somewhat lethal projectiles.

After the summer holidays all the kids brought back to school with them Cobjoe's (Horse Chestnut) to play Conkers with. Most of the Cob Joe's had been soaked in vinegar and then baked to make them harder. Kids would use a nail or other sharp implement to bore the Cob Joe for stringing. I would carefully drill the hole so has not to cause a weak spot. I really don't think it made any difference to the outcome. During battle we would enlist a mediator to ensure that the hit was clean and not jerked. But endless arguments still ensued as to who was the actual winner.

The only time that the lads of Devonshire Street collaborated with the rest of the West End was when we came together to assemble the enormous bonfire that was built by the side of the Tin Mission on the bottom. We would start collecting combustible material some three or four weeks before Bonfire Night. Every night groups of kids took turn to stand guard over the part built structure as rival gangs from Albert Street and areas of Whittington Moor would try to make raiding incursions, as we did likewise with them. Bernard and I always bought Standard Fireworks mainly Penny Bangers and Tupenny Cannon. On one Bonfire Night the group from Devo was stood watching the bonfire when our Bern casually lit a Cannon and slipped in the jacket pocket of 'Spradin' Brown an older lad from Edmund Street yard. Luckily, with the excitement and noise, he was not aware it had been placed there. When the firework exploded other than shock, he was unarmed but it ruined his coat. We all knew the danger of handling lit fireworks as only the year before Tony Coupe, brother of Dorothy had blown off a thumb whilst experimenting with his home made fireworks. Once again our Bern had shown utter disregard to consequence of his actions.

Winter was the season for making 'Winter Warmers.' Basically it was a tin can which had a series of holes punched through it. Attached was a long wire loop that served as a handle. Hot coals from a camp fire were placed in the can which was then swung around to force oxygen on to the coals to cause them to flame. When the fire was nicely going you could place your hands near to the can to get them warm. The best can to use was a Tate and Lyle Golden Syrup tin as it was robust and had a more ideal shape than the normal sized baked bean tin.

A grass hillock locally known as the Futrell is situated along side Kendall Road and just short of the entrance to Levens Way. In the summer of 1944 before Kendall Road or any other building development took place the Futrell dropped away steeply before levelling out as a large, flattish field that reached to the brook bottom. The Futrell formed part of our playing area on the fields beyond our back garden boundary wall. Aping Blood Jones a group of us from Devonshire Street and Racecourse Mount had built a substantive Den into the strata of the Futrill well capable of accommodating all six namely, Bernard, Pete Wright, Freddy Finney, Roger Huckerby, Keith Tasker and I. The Den was constructed by excavating a trench through a lower clay ridge and roofing it with corrugated sheeting supported by trimmed tree branches, the whole then covered over with grass sods. Internally there was a fireplace with a smoke hole drain pipe, below which was a steel tube on which to hang a mashing can used for making hot oxo drinks. It was left open at one end and partially blocked on the other end to ensure a good through draught.

At the top of Devonshire Street there was a fenced footpath which passed by a disused pottery (we called it the clay hole) leading up to Lancaster Road. To the left at the top of the path stood a detached stone built cottage with a substantial vegetable garden belonging to an elderly couple Mr. and Mrs. Tompkins. They were truly nineteenth century characters. He attired in pork pie hat, farmers smock and corded trousers that where tied with string about his lower leg just above his boots. Her with straw hat perched on top a bun style hair dressing that framed a round bespectacled jovial face and attired in pinafore and boots. Their garden was always targeted when we wanted spuds to bake on our camp fire. As was also Davis's orchard, located on Duston Lane when the apples and greengages were ripe.

On one afternoon Pete and I were at the Den when three young men arrived at the futrell. They belonged to a model aircraft flying club and this area had been chosen as an ideal site to launch their models from. Pete and I sat memorised as they gradually assembled their masterpiece creations. The youths talked to each other in a sort of coded jargon that we did not understand using phrases such as 'I need a piece of sixteenth' and 'pass me the cement' All the requests duly materialised from a small tool box. They assembled a rubber powered propeller driven aircraft covered in bright yellow tissue paper stretch tightly over its framework. On launch the plane soared upwards and commenced to make large turning circles until the rubber was unwound. The model then glided smoothly downwards to make a perfect landing. To say the least we were impressed. The other model was a large Sailplane covered with black tissue paper. When launched it held a steady course clearing the brook bottom and continuing over Mason's fields until it disappeared out of sight heading toward Dunston Road some half a mile away. One of the young men set off in pursuit but his search did not locate it as he returned empty handed.

Just after watching the flying display I was sitting on Winnie Wrights front door step with Pete and was talking about how we might build a similar model aeroplane. The afternoon was hot and sunny and we could smell the melting gas tar separating from the pebbles on the road. I think it was Pete who suggested that if we went round the street and collected all the spent match sticks they could be stuck together by the melted tar. We did manage to put together a sort of miss-mash framework but due to the heat the tar would not set. It would be another six years before we built and flew our first Kiel Craft 'Gypsy' model aeroplane.

For quite some time the Den became the favourite focal point of all our activities relegating the back yard as a venue for the occasional meeting with other neighbourhood kids or having the odd game of Rounder's with the girls from Devonshire Street. This was also about the time we formed a football team. Mum purchased some old shirts from a jumble sale and dyed them green. We styled ourselves 'Shamrock Rovers' and played against other local teams from Mountcastle and Albert Streets. The team as I remember was Eric Sheppard, Gerald Hall, Barry Webster, Keith Webster, Desmond Linney, Tommy Hardy, our Bern, Peter Smith, Peter Wright, Me and Keith Tasker. Young Michael Hall was mascot. I have to say we were not very good but if enthusiasm counted we would have won every game.

Before building the Den our dilapidated garden shed had served as a convenient meeting place for the neighbourhood kids during inclement weather. It had a pot bellied stove, work bench and a collection of a few rusty tools. The walls had on them a collection of sepia photographic cards of 1930s footballers. I particularly remember one card of Frank Soo of Stoke City pinned up. Also in the shed were kept two pet 'male' white mice in a make shift wood box with a wire mesh front. Our Bern had obtained these mice by swapping some fag cards for them with Georgy Caddywould from Mountcastle Street. We were surprised but absolutely delighted when they produced a litter of five blind pink babies. Within a three month period we had over seventy mice in ten boxes and could not stop then breeding. Luckily our Bern managed to persuade Frankie Hargreaves a lad from Albert Street to take all the mice in exchange for six Fan Tailed 'Tippler' Pigeons. Eventually when we let the birds fly free they returned to Frankie coop. He returned them to us several times but on each occasion they went back to their 'home' coop. That was the end of our pigeon keeping.

When I watch a particular scene from the film *Saturday Night and Sunday Morning* where Ma Bull is stood in the alley gossiping to a neighbour about Arthur Seaton my mind always goes back to war time hot summer afternoons in Devonshire Street when the heat was so intensified by the density of housing it caused the tarmac road surface to melt which gave off a smell that became intoxicating. On such late afternoons all manner of chair and stool would be brought out on the street and neighbours would sit cheerfully chatting away to each other. The exception was Mrs Seymour an elderly sour faced woman who would stand for hours with her arms folded and sucking in deep breaths of air as she spit out vitriolic gossip to her long suffering neighbour Mrs Pearson about kids on the street in general but me and our Bern in particular. If looks could kill, then we would surely be dead. I cannot ever recall doing anything to her that would warrant this attention. Maybe it was just in her nature to be a nosey busybody who had nothing better to do with her time. This small street was a stage that comedy, pathos and drama were played out on a daily basis for all to view;

Edith Kennel with daughter Brenda 1952

Edith Kennel had nowt, but you could not pass her house without having her last slice of bread and jam stuffed in your mitt. She was a fiercely proud and independent person who I am sure starved herself in order to ensure her kids did not go without sustenance. Edith was so destitute that she could not muster the few rags that would enable her youngest Roland to get a balloon off Freddy Ashmore the local rag and bone man. Freddy, from travelling stock, was the archetype young Harold Steptoe with his flat cap, red cotton neck scarf, tweed overcoat and wellies who always had a twinkle in his roguish eyes as he bartered from his cart drawn by a skewbald pony call Tim. Young Roland had proffered Freddy a single piece of cloth about the size of a kerchief hoping to exchange it for a balloon, and on Freddy's refusal, went indoors crying. Edith was also very sensitive of her status and reacted to this rebuff as a personal insult. There followed an altercation between Edith and Freddy which was then adjoined by Edith's dog Mac, which proceeded to savage Freddy's trouser leg. On hearing the ruckus, Edith's eldest daughter Mary, who was home on leave from the NAAFI, stuck her head out of an upstairs unglazed window aperture and shouted in a rather affected accent 'Come in mother, and bring that bloody well dog with you.' Freddy who knew Edith so well retorted with his usual cheeky quip; 'Yes, and shut that kennel door behind you.' It was much like a scene from Old Mother Riley played out by Arthur Lucan and Kitty McShane but much funnier because it was played out live on Devonshire Street. Of course Edith would not have seen it that way.

Edith was always hard up and flitted from shop to shop to try to reduce her grocery bill. When told the Co-op on Whittington Moor paid out a dividend to members she immediately registered and proceeded to run up a bill. A fortnight later when asked by the manager for settlement she told him; 'take it out of the divi.'

All the houses on Devonshire Street were cold and draughty, having one open fire for heating, but in winter time the bedrooms were like ice boxes and you would need several layers of blankets and old coats to get a modicum of warmth which was also supplemented by heated black leaded bricks wrapped in a towel to keep your feet warm. Edith's bedrooms were lacking a great many window panes and we would often be disturbed at night listening to the kids screams of suffering from exposure to the freezing temperature conditions that swept unhindered through their room.

Colin Glossop, a senior school friend who lived at Cutthorpe, came to stay with us one weekend and asked me quite innocently;' who owns that warehouse?' 'What warehouse?' I asked. 'That one,' he said, pointing to Edith Kennel's house. To his great disbelief I had to explain to him that it was residential property, for he thought that I was kidding him.

It was from Freddy Ashmore that we got our Oscar. Freddy mostly traded yellow chicks, and from experience we knew that they were usually cock birds. On one occasion among the yellow chicks he had on his cart there was a lone sooty black chick that had taken Mums fancy. Freddy swore blind that it was a hen and wanted double the normal weight of rags for it. Mum eventually got the chick by giving Freddy an old overcoat that we used as extra bedding in winter. She named the chick Oscar. We had only had Oscar a few days when on the Sunday dinner time he jumped into the gravy boat full of scalding hot liquid and severely burned himself. He was helplessly flapping around and Mum was panic stricken shouting; 'Do something, do something.' I picked up the bedraggled bungle, ran out the back, and hurled it at the wall with all the might I could muster. The chick lay still for a moment then miraculously stood up and hobbled into the kitchen to its water bowl. Our Oscar started laying eggs some two months after the incident and apart from having a permanent limp lived a happy and productive life.

Winnie Wright's door seemed to be permanently open and we would stand against an oilcloth table spread that drew you to it with its wonderful aroma of margarine like smell. Winnie was very easy going and seemed oblivious to the hordes of kids that gathered in her house. Although on one occasion, she must have been feeling off the hooks for she said to our Bern 'Can't you stand in the jennel?' To which he replied 'Its cold and its rainin.' Winnie was always coming round to our house to beg a cup of sugar. Mum could never understand why the Wright's used so much sugar, the explanation was that it was their favourite fare to have bread, margarine and sugar sandwiches for which I also got a liking.

Winnie's husband Arthur was in Burma doing service with the 14th Army which at that time were fighting a bitter campaign against the Japanese. Winnie would often go out for a drink with her friend Kit Bond who lived further down the street. One such occasion a group of kids had gathered in Winnie's to play 'truth or dare,' Winnie's daughter Betty was 'dared' to take our Bernard in the wall cupboard that was built into the chimney breast recess for a kiss and cuddle, which they did. Whilst they were in the cupboard Winnie and Kit arrived back earlier than expected, the reason was that they had arranged to have a late night card session with a few others from the West End that they had met in the Devonshire Hotel, a public house on Occupation Road. There was a mad scramble by us kids to exit the house but Betty and Bernard could not get out of the cupboard in time. And there they stayed until the card school broke up some hours later

Dorris Wright and Ray Herrod – Blackpool 1949

Winnie's eldest daughter Doris was a glamorous teenager who modelled her looks on the film star Betty Grable, and her friend, Ethel Kennel, daughter of Edith, resembled a young Esther Williams the swimming film star. At that time female hosiery was nigh on impossible to obtain so it was a common sight on the back yard to see them both rubbing red builder sand on their legs then use a black eyebrow pencil to mark in the seams. Doris in particular used to tease the local youths. On one occasion she was stood at the open window of their back bedroom when three young men, who had been labouring all day at Mason's farm, climbed over the back wall as a short cut to the West End. Doris attracted the attention of Billy Bunting, Louise Sims and Malcolm Grattage by pretending to do a strip tease. Billy who lived in a yard at the top of Devonshire Street quickly obtained a ladder and all three youths attired in dirty bib and brace overalls and wellies covered in cow dung climbed the ladder and entered the bedroom. Doris meanwhile had made her escape through the front door and ran down to Kit Bond's house dressed only in her under slip. Ethel went on to become an excellent swimmer, I am not sure if it was inspired by seeing Esther Williams, but for one, I was beholding to her later when we both joined the British Railways Swimming Club. On which matters I will discuss later.

At Christmas time 1945 Arthur returned from Burma and was given heroes welcome home party that lasted well into the early hours. At that party Arthur made a present to me of his battered old slouch hat that he had worn all through the Burma Campaign which I treasured for many years. Arthur found normal civilian life difficult to cope with and resorted to unorthodox methods to barely scrape a living. His main pre-occupation was catching wild birds in Sheepbridge woods using a sticky substance called birdlime that glued their feet to a roosting branch. Although it was strictly illegal there was a great demand for wild birds, especially bullfinches He kept these wild birds in his back bedroom and on one occasion our Bern and Roger Huckerby sneaked up Wright's stairs and set twenty bullfinches free. Arthur went ballistic but never did find out who were the culprits that had cost him a considerable loss of income. Arthur together with Wilf Sims from Racecourse Mount and Jack Taylor from Arundal Road regularly poached rabbits from Barlow Game wood, and on the day following, the putrid stench of rotting giblets, that had been dumped over Wright's back wall, permeated the whole street. The same three would carry out a night raid on the orchard at Grovehill on St Johns Road, the home of Dr Sutcliffe, and carry off sack loads of ripe fruit. Throughout this period Arthur often suffered severe bouts of malaria which would eventually lead to a premature death.

'Old Lass' Aldred would always have a cup of tea ready for me when I walked up the street from school and would insist that I went into her front room to drink it whilst sitting on her settee. At first I though she was trying to poison me as we regarded her as some kind of demented witch. Once again this thought is always recalled when I am watching a particular scene from the film *Hue and Cry* were a young lad Joe (Harry Fowler) is offered a drink of 'ginger pop,' which he thinks has been poised by Felix H Wilkinson (Alastair Sim) a crank comic book writer who Joe was visiting... It turned out that Mrs Aldred knew Mum was not at home at that time of the day and this was an act of kindness on her part. I often dropped in on Mrs Aldred to keep her company as I suspect she was a lonely old soul. We became quite good friends although when our Albert, a bantam cock, disappeared she swore blind that she had not see him despite Billy Bunting telling Mum her dustbin was full of feathers.

A regular and kid's favourite visitor to the street on Sunday dinner time was a real wise cracking chap called Les who sold Mellor's icecream from a hand cart. He would always park his cart outside the same house and after serving all the kids with a rather watery concoction would say 'Well its time for dinner, just keep an eye on me cart. I won't be long' and disappear inside the house. Within minutes the cart would be surround by kid's barging each other out the way in an attempt to reach into the ice tub. The bedroom window would then open and Les's face would appear. 'Clear off you little bugger's,' he would shout down to us. The whole street knew that he had not really gone in for his dinner as the husband of the house was still in the Devonshire Hotel having his pre-dinnertime drink.

Bernard and I dreaded the Sunday mornings earmarked for our hair cutting. Reg Sylvester from the top of the street would come to our house and 'cut' our hair with a pair of shears that had several teeth missing. Dad would insist that Reg gave us a real close crop to save money by prolonging his next visit. I would sit in trepidation watching the shears biting into our Bernard's scalp fetching blood and hearing his winches of pain that were admonished with severe looks from Dad who would dab his head with iodine in between cuts which caused him to winch in greater pain. Unfortunately despite my pleading I never escaped this ritual torture.

Charlie (Wag) Mellors at Devonshire Street

Our house was known by all the kids of Devonshire Street and Racecourse Mount as a place were you could always get a bit of 'snap.' There was home made bread and meat or bacon doorstops to be had, with a glass of Clayton's lemonade in summer, and mugs of oxo pobbs in winter to swig it down with. The kitchen became a play area during inclement weather where pillow fights and other boisterous games took place. We made a drinks cabinet out of an old beer crate which was hung on the wall and was stocked with lemonade and Tizer

Mrs Mellors with granddaughter Marjorie age 2 years at Devonshire Street 1939

which we would mixed together to make a cocktail complete with glace cherry just like we had seen at the Lyceum.

At number 30 there lived Charlie 'Wag' Mellors and his wife Harriet; a remarkable couple who were bringing up two of their grandchildren, Daisy and Marjorie, the children of Rose their daughter.

Daisy was a strikingly beautiful girl whose delicate disposition precluded her from playing out on the street and sadly would die at the very young age of nineteen. Marjorie eight years junior to Daisy had slight learning problems, and consequently, was fiercely protected by her grandparents who had to contend with the day to day systematic bullying of their granddaughter. Everything about her made her a target for the cruelties young adolescents delight in inflicting on those who are shy, sensitive or different, regretful to say, her tormentors included Bernard and me. Marjorie now in her seventy second year (at the time of writing) resides in the same locality of my brother and they often talk of the 'old times' and remarkably she holds no grudge of her treatment in the West End, indeed she looks back on that time with great fondness. Marjorie told my brother that when her grandparents were deceased 'nobody wanted her' and she was placed in Whittington Hall for a period of some thirty years before she met and married her dear husband Donald.

Daisy Mellors 1948

When our Bern mentioned that I was currently writing a memoir of Devonshire Street she kindly supplied some of her treasured photographs and memories for inclusion in this book, for which I am indebted to her. If you eventually read this book Marjorie, thank you for your generous spirit.

Georgy Willis together with his mother, or maybe wife, I was never sure which, lived in the bottom yard of Devonshire Street that was accessed off lower Mountcastle Street. He had some how got hold of a 'pet' Spider Monkey which back then was as rare as 'hen's teeth' therefore it was quite a sort out curiosity, and a treat for us kids to watch it leap about in their front room. The monkey was vicious and prone to biting visitors and was not house trained so there was pooh everywhere. Sad to say it did not survive very long for whilst swinging on the live light flex it bit through it and electrocuted itself, and in so doing blacked out all the properties in the yard.

Wilf Sims of Racecourse Mount made a living by foraging bits and pieces from a land fill site colloquially known a Barlow 'Shit' Tip and also the Chesterfield Borough Cleansing Department at Stonegravels. He would be especially on the lookout for bicycle parts that he, together with Reg Silvester, could rebuild and sell second-hand. Dad bought such a hybrid for thirty shillings from them as a birthday present for our Bern. It had a Rudge frame with rod actuated brakes and a Sturmey-Archer three speed fixed wheel hub gear. Overnight it had been gloss painted with Chinese Lacquer in a vivid purple colour, and of course our Bern could not wait to try it out. Like most cheap paint in them days it really needed several days to harden and dry. Mum spent most of his birthday rubbing down our Bern with margarine trying to remove purple paint from his arm's, leg's and even in his hair, but the paint seemed impervious to all her effort. He looked as though he had a severe case of scabies.

Dad usually had a ulterior motive when he bought us anything out of the ordinary, the bike was a prime example, as he used it every day to go to work on, relegating our Bern use to Saturday afternoon's and Sundays. Mrs Newbold, the grandmother of Barry and Keith Webster, who lived opposite us ran a 'twenty week' Christmas catalogue club which me and our Bern always joined. You chose an item and the cost was divided into twenty weekly payments. There would be great excitement when the items were delivered the week before Christmas. One year our Bern chose an ARP Lamp. This hooded torch was a standard bicycle lamp modified for use in the blackout. The hood prevented the light shining upward but gave a good light span around the feet. Just after Christmas Dad hack sawed the hood off so he could personally use it on Bernard's bike. Our Bern was heartbroken.

Chapter 7 – That's Entertainment

For in and out, above, about, below,

'Tis nothing but a Magic

Shadow-Show,

Played in a Box whose

Candle is the Sun,

Round which we Phantom

Figures come and go

RUBA IYAT OF OMAR KHAYYAM

Dad & Esme on back field at Devonshire Street 1946

During the war our local cinema the Lyceum was well attended with queuing being the norm. Our family normally went to the Saturday night first showing at 5.30pm. We were always accompanied by our Esme but on one particular Saturday summer evening our 'Es', who had earlier been to Sheffield with her Aunt Gert, arrived too late at Devonshire Street to go with us. Thinking that she could let herself into the house with the backdoor key, kept under the dustbin, she entered the back yard through the gate and was immediately attacked by our Bantam cock Albert who was loose in the yard. 'The little bleeder kept fluttering up to my chest trying to peck my eyes out. 'A terrified and sobbing Esme told us after Dad rescued her from the lavatory where she had sort refuge and had been imprisoned for nearly two hours. Mum had to give her a 'dab' wash and change of knickers has she had 'wet' the one's she was wearing. I remember as a special treat to 'revive' our Es, all three of us kids were each given a steaming mug of Bovril before our Es commandeered our bed leaving me and Bern to sleep on the floor in our parents bedroom.

On week nights there was only one show and the cinema was closed on Sunday. There were two changes of films weekly. If we were lucky we may get to see an extra film on a Thursday night as the general price of admission was only sixpence. As a special treat we may get to see the Saturday afternoon 2pm matinee especially screened for the younger children with admission price of three pence. With a full attendance of 650 noisy kids from all over Newbold and Whittington Moor the commissionaire 'Bobby' Teazle tried valiantly to maintain order by using a long cane to poke rowdy offenders which only served to provoke even more noise from their pals. The usual film fare was the western singing cowboys Gene Autry and Roy Rogers. But I preferred the more realistic Ray'Crash'Corrigan and Charles Starrett as the black masked avenger The Durango Kid with his white horse Raider. On the comedy slapstick side there was the very funny Three Stooges, Shemp, Larry and Moe and the East Side Kids with Huntz Hall, later to emerge as the incomparable Bowery Boys with Leo

Gorcy as Mugsy. The film that I remember with particular sadness was *'Buffalo Bill'* with Joel McCrea taking the title role but was out shone by the fine acting of Anthony Quinn as the young Cheyenne War Chief Yellow Hand. I was always on the side of the Indians now known as Native Americans. The climax of the film was a fight to the death between the once childhood friends Bill Cody and Yellow Hand. Of course I knew what the outcome would be. When we played at Cowboys and Indians there was Keith Tasker and me who wanted to be Indians and two would argue who was going to be Crazy Horse, War Chief of the Sioux Nation, Keith and I were avid readers of Combat Comic Books which featured the adventures of Black Hawk the Fearless Sioux Warrior and would go halves to buy the latest issue each Saturday. We would for many years pronounce Sioux as sihox only much later to discover it was pronounced sue.

We as a group graduated to become ABC Minors at the Regal on a Saturday mornings at 10am.the admission price being sixpence. I well remember the inaugural meeting where we were given an introductory talk by two inappropriate dressed representatives of Associated British Cinema's, a gentleman in black tie and dress suit and a glamorously lady in sequinned gown who then taught us how to sing The ABC Minors Song by following the words projected on the screen and sung to the tune 'Blaze Away';

We are the boys and girls well known as

Minors of the ABC

And every Saturday all line up

To see the films we like

And shout aloud with glee

We like to laugh and have a singsong

Such a happy crowd are we

We're all pals together

The minors of the ABC

After this introduction we were all invited to become members and each received a membership card, florescent badge and assigned our very own seats. Ours were in Block Twenty. It was very slick marketing on part of the proprietors of Associated British Cinemas as it was designed to make you feel you belong to an idealistic extended family, which of course we really never did.

The appeal to us was the programmes themselves. Firstly every week there was always a cliff hanger serial such as '*Don Winslow of the Navy*' and follow on series '*Don Winslow of the Coast Guard*.' Don Winslow the eponymous hero, would single handed grappled with saboteurs, and later take on a whole Japanese Imperial Marine Company to save his homeland from peril. We also viewed many exciting films but the two that made a lasting impression on me were '*The Fighting Lady*' about the aircraft carrier Enterprise who participated in every major action of the Pacific war, and '*The Fighting Sullivan's*' a true story about five brothers who all perished whilst serving together in the US forces during the early part of the war. The latter really touched me deeply as the story centred on the youngest brother who would always be trying to keep up with his other brothers and kept shouting 'Wait for me'. I identified with the younger brother as being my own situation within our gang. The melodrama at the films end was when the eldest brother who could have saved himself went back to try to free his trapped youngest brother and consequently they died together. After this tragedy The US congress made a special law that forbade siblings serving together in the armed forces.

I did mention that queuing for the cinema was quite normal but when the film *Ali Baba and the Forty Thieves* was released me and our Bern were disappointed to be confronted by an enormous crowd outside the Lyceum for the first Saturday evening showing. It was apparent that we would not get in the cinema. Bernard crawled through a maze of legs all the way to the front of the queue which had formed down a long entrance tunnel to the cheap seats. He then started to cry and told the waiting people that I had been separated from him by the crush of people. The message reached the back of the queue and I was allowed safe passage way through by the sympathetic crowd.

By this time we were going to the pictures on our own. When an 'A' certificate film was being shown, we like many other small boys, would wait outside the cinema for a grown ups to come along ask 'Will you take us in?' After they took you in they'd usually go and sit somewhere else, if not, then we our selves would. We never needed adults to take us into the Corporation Cinema in Chesterfield which was the main venue for Tarzan films starring Johnny Weissmuller who we all idolised and was our role model when re-enacting his exploits in Sheepbridge and Duston woods.

The tunes of 1944 had a certain upbeat optimism following D Day 6th June reflected in such songs as; *When They Sound The Last All Clear* (Vera Lynn), *When The Lights Go On Again* (Issy Bonn) *The Homecoming Waltz* (Donald Peers) and Alan Breeze with Billy Cotton and his Band's *I'm Going to Get Lit Up*. Of the many memorable films of the period was *Stage Door Canteen, For Whom the Bell Tolls, Going My Way* and *Buffalo Bill* with propaganda war films; *Bataan, The Fighting Seabees* and *Millions Like Us*.

In December of 1944 the popular American Dance Band leader Major Glenn Miller was in an aircraft that was lost over the English Channel.

We listened on the radio to *Happidrome* with Harry Korris 'We three in Happidrome, working for the BBC, Ramsbottom and Enoch and Me' And Tommy Handley's ITMA with Mrs Mopp 'Can I do you now, sir?' Colonel Chinstrap 'I don't mind if I do.' And Ali Oop 'I go-I come back.' We would listen expectantly awaiting the pounding theme tune Coronation Scot which introduced the serialised 'Paul Temple' mysteries which would remain a favourite for another five years.

On Friday nights at about this time we as a family started going to the Hippodrome on Corporation Street. The Hippodrome was a live performance variety theatre. I found most of the acts were beyond my comprehension, and consequently boring. Although I can still recall two acts that left an impression on me. I was awe struck that a large monkey could perform complicated acrobatic feats on its own. I was disappointed to be told that it was just a man in a monkey costume. The second act is still most vivid in my mind being a young female contortionist who finished her act standing on her hand having her torso and legs over her back and head and drinking a red coloured liquid from a wine glass held between her feet. In the early fifties I went to the Hippodrome, with a work colleague Peter Brown, to see Jane the Daily Mirror forces pin up and of strip cartoon fame. She appeared in a variety of poses in a flimsy costume using a little dachshund dog called Fritz to stragically cover her modesty. We must have really enjoyed the act as we later went to see Phyllis Dixey billed as the 'Queen of Striptease.' She must have been approaching 60 years old by then but she was a real trouper. Sadly, soon after this visit, the theatre closed in 1955.

Chapter 8 – Towards Peacetime

Hundreds of dewdrops to greet the dawn,
Hundreds of bees in the purple clover,
Hundreds of butterflies on the lawn,
but only one mother the wide world over.

GEORGE COOPER

Only One Mother

Mum at parents house 47 Racecourse Road
1946

In late 1944 our Jack was released from the Royal Corps of Transport to enable him to be involved with Dadad's Mod contract of re-cycling war surplus vehicles. This meant that Mum could now leave the heavy work at the Yard but she still had to go up to Nin's on two evenings a week which would continue until 1951.To offset the loss of earnings at the Yard Dadad had arranged for Mum to be re-employed as a part time seamstress by Harry Fish a Chesterfield Furrier who was a personal friend, and both him and Barney Goodman tailored Dadad's suits. Back then wearing real fur was not viewed as being politically incorrect but was haute couture. Harry Fish had his business near the bottom of Saltergate next to the Shakespeare Inn. Just around the corner on Hollywell Street was the 'Hygienic' Bakery were every Saturday morning after work Mum would buy me and our Bern a scrumptious cream slice pastry each.

Taking about cream buns reminds me of an occasion that our Jack took our Bernard with him whilst visiting Jim Bullions a professional football player on the books of Derby County who had a second hand car business at Shuttlewood. They then went down the road to the home of Harry Whitford at Calow Green. Harry was a manager at Ryland Works in Chesterfield and had many dealings with Dadad. Every Christmas on the behest of Dadad, Harry would get one of his staff to make two toy Cars or Lorries as presents for me and Bernard. Mrs Whitford must have been taken up with our Bern's angelic looks for she took him in her kitchen and made him a present of six iced buns which she put in a brown paper bag. Bernard dashed back to the car closely followed by our Jack. 'Gis a bun Bernard' he said. 'I can't I've ett um Jack' replied our Bernard whilst stuffing his mouth full of buns. 'You greedy little varmint, you ort to choke on em' said our Jack whilst grabbing him round the throat and shaking him violently. After Jack stopped shaking him our Bern said; 'we'll they were mine.'

Mum really enjoyed the social company of the all female staff at Harry Fish and they became more like an extended family to me and Bernard sending birthday cards and Easter eggs and such like. This was encouraged by Harry and his wife Lilly who would invite all the Staffs children and younger relatives to parties held at their home at Cobden Road.

I recall vividly one particular birthday part held for their young son David. It was still war time and food was not only on ration but was also scarce. The party fare for fifteen children was set in the opulent dining room and consisted of all manner of pastries, sweetmeats, jellies, trifles ice creams and six birthday cakes that celebrated each year of David's life. The party was then followed by fun and games in their beautiful garden orchestrated by Harry. As we took our leave Harry gave each child a handful of silver three penny pieces, which I still have in my possession. I have been to many parties since then but have never enjoyed any so much as that magical afternoon at Cobden Road.

Mum had been working for Harry Fish for nearly three years when she started having trouble with her right eye which was diagnosed has having a corneal ulcer. Mum had to attend the Royal Hospital on several occasions for treatment which consisted of actually scraping the ulcerated part, bit by bit, from her eye. On these occasions I accompanied Mum as after the scraping her eye was bandaged and she was severely disoriented as a result of the treatment. Due to her impaired eye sight she was no longer able to work as a seamstress so Harry Fish offered her alternate employment as a domestic assistant to Mrs Sadler, his housekeeper and mother-in-law. Mum was for the next four years treated more of a companion than an employee by Mrs Sadler and both Harry and Lilly held her in high esteem and she also became a surrogate mother to David as Lily worked full time in the shop. Mum was privy to the entire goings on at Cobden Road and related to us an extraordinary happening;

One eventful weekend a group of men with cockney accents booked into the Shakespeare Inn then proceeded to break through the dividing wall and stole Harry's most valuable stock of mink coats worth many hundred's of pounds. It was really hilarious when some months later a similar group of men pertaining to be musicians booked into the Shakespeare one Friday evening. The landlord was suspicious has they did not appear to have any musical instruments. He alerted the police who when interviewing the men were told that they were part of the Morton Frazier Harmonic Group booked to play the Hippodrome on Saturday evening. On their request the police phone Harry Fish who informed them that they were indeed bona fide and that Morton Frazier, his brother, was staying the weekend at Cobden Road. Mum said this fiasco really lifted the gloom of the break in which had cost Harry a great deal of pain and expense.

When Harry Fish retired and was leaving the district he ensured that Mum would not have the hardship of being out of work by recommending her services to Evelyn Portman who worked as a pharmaceutical area representative for Robinson & Sons. Evelyn, a spinster, lived with her mother at Littlemoor and was away from home for long periods. Mrs Portman was a delightful lady who always made me and Bernard most welcome when we had occasion to visit. Mum worked for Evelyn for nearly three years before sadly, Mrs Portman died. Evelyn sold the house and rented a flat in Cutthorpe an annex of Eukin's Farm who had been the supplier of milk to the Portman's. Evelyn suggested Mum for employment with the Royal Hospital as a ward domestic cleaner and supplied an excellent reference in support of Mum's application. Mum worked on the Private Patients Ward until her retirement in 1975.

By mid 1944 my Dad had long since stopped growing vegetables and had turned the garden over to keeping poultry, namely Bantams. We had six hens and one cockerel named Albert. They were free range but nested and roosted in the shed. He also at this time went into partnership to keep pigs with 'Bras' Smith and Tom Blissett, two of his greyhound racing buddies The pigs were housed in a rented cattle stall at Manny Taylor's yard on King Street, Whittington Moor. Manny kept geese and turkeys in the yard which were free ranging and fiercely territorial. Me and Bern were intimidated by the appearance of the turkeys and by the aggression of the geese and dreaded the times when it was our turn to muck out and feed the pigs. We would creep up to the entrance, wait for an opportunity, then dash pell-mell down the yard and dive headlong over the stall door. Getting back out wasn't as easy as the geese would hang around the stall for what seemed to us like an eternity before giving an opportunity for escape. By Christmas time when the time came for the pigs to go to a local butcher for slaughter none of the partners could let them go as they had become more like pets than pork. They kept them a further year before cutting their losses and selling them to Bill Hewitt a farmer from New Whittington who also owned and raced greyhounds at Wheeldon Mill. Selling the pigs came as a great relief for Bern and I.

The war in Europe came to an end on 7th May1945. This joyful news gradually leaked out during the day but was not confirmed until the next day 8th May which was called 'VE Day' and was declared a national holiday. I remember that it was a dismal rainy morning that saturated the street decorations of flags and bunting, but it did not quell the enthusiasm as the whole street spontaneously arranged a kiddie's street party for that afternoon. Tables and chairs were brought out into the street and every family contributed what little they had to make it a most memorable day.

The highlight of the afternoon was a spectacular tap dancing routine by the nine year old Eunice Smith dressed as a toy soldier in gold tunic and a tall braided black Grenadier's hat, the likes of which I had never seen. Eunice was not a street resident, hailing from Pottery Lane, but kindly appeared by popular request and arranged by her brother Alf Smith who was at that time living on Devonshire Street.

After the party the older folk were dancing to an old windup horn gramophone belonging to Reg Silvester. The street party wound up by everyone doing the Conga up Devonshire Street, across Racecourse Mount then down Arundel Road were on the bottom by the Tin Mission a bonfire was lit and the whole of the West End partied to the early hours.

By 1945 Mum had registered our family with Hicks Retail Grocery Shop at the bottom of Scarsdale Road. Hicks a grocery store of the old type with marble-topped counters, shining brass scales and weights and Manager and assistant wearing clean white aprons. Very few items were pre-wrapped, so we could see butter being weighed out and patted into shape with wooden butter-pats, and then expertly wrapped in grease-proof paper. Cheese was cut from a large block, using a wire cheese-cutter with wooden handles. Sugar was already in packets which were actually always of blue paper (sugar paper?) Biscuits were displayed in large cubical tins with a glass panel in the lid so that the customer could see and choose the desired biscuits which were then taken out of the tin by the assistant, weighed and put into a paper bag. Tea which could only be obtained in loose leaf form was one of the few items to be sold pre-wrapped as nowadays. Tea bags were not introduced until 1953 by Tetley's and did not become popular until the mid sixty's.

In 1945 Hicks Grocery Store was managed by Miss Vardy a typical middle aged Edwardian type spinster, attired in high necked blouse, ankle length skirt and button up shoes. Her dark hair was swept up from the nape into a top knot with two side ringlets. What was noticeable about her was she always wore pince-nez eye-glasses on the end of her nose above which piercing blue eyes held you in a hypnotic gaze. She had an assistant, Bob Hayes, who would a year later become manager. I recall an occasion when our family visited Miss Vardy's home at Wellington Street, New Whittington to view a settee she had for sale. Her front room was furnished with all sorts of Victoriana items and heavy chintz soft furnishings. I remember her asking if we would like 'refreshments' and

Mum said a cup of tea would be nice. Miss Vardy employed a young girl of maybe sixteen, or seventeen, as a domestic help and 'companion' who she directed to 'put the kettle on.' Miss Vardy after setting out, what to my apprehension, looked like very expensive crockery went to the cutlery drawer and to her chagrin discovered that two knives had been replaced back in a crossed position. There followed an unbelievable verbal regaling of the poor unfortunate girl, who just stood there petrified. I could not comprehend the callous nature of this attack for such a trivial thing and ever after I held her in low esteem.

After Miss Vardy's retirement Bob Hayes took over as manager of Hicks, with his wife as assistant. One particular morning I was with Mum in the shop when she asked Bob's wife; 'Have you got any breadeva?' To Mums annoyance I kept asking: 'What's breadeva, what's breadeva?' And kept getting a 'shoosh' in reply. Out side the shop I was still inquisitive, hoping that it may be some kind of a new 'treat' for me and our Bern that she wanted to keep secret as a surprise. To my utter disappointment she explained that Bob's wife was called Eva. Most of the stock at Hicks was kept in a back room which gave me and our Bern, when shopping on our own, opportunity to do a bit of shop lifting. We would take anything that lay to hand. I remember one instance when we stole a packet of processed dates which neither of us cared for. It wasn't until much later that Mum explained to us that she and Bob had an arrangement that he added everything 'stolen' to her bill. Bob was one of nature's gentlemen and never ever 'shopped us.' We as kids were not aware that he was very ill, for he never complained, but sadly he died quite young.

Whittington Moor in the 1940s and early 1950s was a thriving centre that provided almost every need from shops, doctors and entertainment. The two largest retail outlets were Derbyshire's and the Co-op both of which had overhead wire and trolleys systems that sent money from point of sale to cashiers office. Receipts and change was returned in the same manner. Derbyshire's was a department store that stocked every conceivable item, and I would stand enthralled as I watched the overhead metal cylinders zip at high speed to and fro across each department. Our nearest chemist was Elliot's situated on Sheffield Road across from Manknell Road and at a corner of a jitty that connected to Station Road. This chemist served our Doctors Sheffield Road Surgery, situated between Manknell Road and Scarsdale Road. Our usual Doctors were MacPharland, Duthie, Jeffries and Dornan. They had rather an attractive receptionist who was to be the object of a rather amusing comment. Mum had a cousin Tommy Lister who lived on Racecourse Mount. Tommy was nearer our age than Mums and would often visit us. On one occasion Mum asked him if he was courting to which he replied; 'Yes I am going out with Muriel. You know, Dr Dornan's receptionist, her with the thin hair and big thighs.' Yes that was typical of Tommy. He once was demonstrating to our family the technique of 'the fireman's lift' using me as the dummy. He had on a loose knitted cardigan and when he stooped to return me to the floor my teeth got caught up in the web like material. When we finally got untangled I found that one of my front teeth was missing.

I remember Mum had seen an article about the latest makeup trends in the Red Letter magazine and was particularly interested in a lipstick called 'Burnt Orange.' Back then all lipstick was vivid pink so this new shade was quite an adventurous and daring departure. Mum sent me down to Elliot's to enquire if they stocked this new shade of lipstick. The obliging assistant spent at least half an hour searching in vain, and in the process got her white overall covered in dust, before suggesting that I try Twelves Chemist at the corner of Queens Street. Mr Twelves, son Reg, and his assistant pharmacist Miss Bort, were all on duty as I asked if they stocked Max Factor's Burnt Orange lipstick. Again they went to extraordinary lengths to oblige and eventually came up with a lipstick by Gala of London that I thought had last seen daylight in the 1920s called 'Orange Glow'. Twelves did not know how to price it so to my great delight, and relief, they offered it free of charge. On application Mums lips took on the colour of tanned leather shoe soles, but to her credit she persevered with it for a few days, for I suspect, it was because she had put so many people about and did not want to lose face.

Twelves the Chemist served the patients of Queen Street surgery, the practice of Dr. Sutcliffe. Later this surgery would also be the practice of Dr. Tait whose expertise I would be thankful for on the occasion of an accident involving my bicycle. I was walking my bicycle down the back yard and slipped in a puddle of soapy water left after Win Wright had been washing. One of the brake levers pierced my right eyebrow and upper lid causing a large gash from which blood was spurting out. Joe Hall our next door neighbour witnessed the accident and immediately applied a compress using a towel. He then carried me all the way down to Queens Street where I was attended to by Dr. Tait, not my own doctor as our surgery on Sheffield Road was not open. I can still envisage Dr. Tait threading a curved needle and then sewing up the wound and applying a dressing. He then gave Joe and me a lift back to Devonshire Street in his car where he reassured Mum that my sight had not been impaired. He then gave Mum advice on further medication that he then prescribed. Dr. Tait visited us on numerous occasions and also by protocol informed our own surgery. Mum was gratified by the kindness and genuine concern shown by Dr. Tait that she re-registered with him and he was her doctor until his retirement in the 1980s.

There were several fish and chip shops in and around Whittington Moor. Nin always used Bodens on Occupation Road. Their son Peter was a friend of Eric 'Blackie' Shaw who was later a work colleague of mine. Both were regular swimmers at Stand Road pool where they displayed a talent for diving off the twenty foot high diving board. After visiting the Lyceum we would call at Laura's Chip Shop, which was situated next door to the cinema, where our Bern and I always received an extra free helping of fish bits. I always associate Laura with the film of the same name which we viewed at the Lyceum, I think, in 1945. It starred Gene Tierney in the title role supported by Clifton Webb and Dana Andrews. It featured a memorable haunting theme tune by David Raksin that I now have in my karaoke catalogue. Dick Cellars also had a chip shop down Duke Street, which is still trading. Our favourite chip shop was Tommy Herring's at the top School Road at a junction with Sheffield Road. B.R. Mills Transport was located behind the Bell School with access off School Road and when visiting Dad at work our treat was fish and chips from Tommy's. Disappointingly, a little later the shop was demolished when my Mothers Uncle Bernard Lister built the present building as a car show room.

Our favourite shop was Wards Cycle Shop on the corner of Avenue Road and Sheffield Road. When eventually we acquired bicycles the store was a virtual cornucopia of spare parts, accessories, paint and transfer's all avidly sought after by the kids from Devonshire Street. It also stocked a tantalising range of Meccano Outfits in their attractive red cardboard boxes that had a picture on the lid of a boy and father building an enormous crane called a 'block setter'. I think it was Christmas 1945 when excitedly I eventually received a Meccano Outfit Number 1A. Neither Mum nor I was aware that this was a conversion set turning a number 1 outfit into a number 2 and was not intended to be used on its own. It was in-comprehensive to me how I was expected to build any of the models show in the instruction book with the supplied contents of two perforated plates, four perforated strips, two angle brackets and, a few nuts and bolts and a hank of green string. I do remember that I proudly displayed to my parents and then to Peter Wright my 'Meccano' sledge, comprising a bent up plate with string loop for pulling it. Throughout the following years I eventually built up my Meccano to a size ten but never was able to build that 'block setter' pictured on the lid of my number 1A outfit.

Chapter 9 – Primary School

And did those feet in ancient times

Walk upon England's mountains green.

WILLIAM BLAKE

Jerusalem

Dad at Skegness 1947

The surrender of the Japanese on Wednesday 15th August 1945, the day known as VJ Day, or Victory over Japan Day, finally brought World War Two to a close. I believe the two days following VJ Day were declared a National Holiday for I remember feeling somehow cheated as we were already on summer holidays from school. With there being no further danger of bombing Dad began to travel further afield to visit different dog racing tracks and regularly took the train or bus to Sheffield to attend venues at Darnall, Owlerton and Hyde Park as well as his weekly visits to Wheeldon Mill. The Saturday after VJ Day Dad took the whole family to Sheffield. It was very exciting for it was the first time either me or Bernard had travelled on a train. On arrival in Sheffield we walked across from the Midland Station to Pond Street were Dad took his leave of us as he was going to spend the afternoon at the Hyde Park dog racing track. As was usual Mum and we kids were left to our own devices. In the event we spent a really lovely afternoon exploring Fitzalan Square, the High Steet and Fargate visiting lots of shops including a really large Woolworth's store, then having a meal in a special local authority British Restaurant where we had a three course meal for nine pence each. The sweet was an impressive pink blancmange that intrigued me by its perfectly circular shape. I now know it had been made in a mould.

In late August Mum and Dad booked us all to go on a day trip to Skegness which would be our first outing to the Seaside. On a Sunday Morning we all set off excitedly on an East Midland service bus. The bus was not designed for comfort having sparsely upholstered leather seat and suspension that shook your spine at every bump in the road. The weather on that Sunday was warm and sunny making us impatient to arrive at the sea side and I recall that about every ten minutes I would ask Dad; 'Are we were there yet?'

The journey did seem to take an eternity and when the bus finally arrived, it was to a vast, drab concreted area, and the bus parked along side what seemed like hundred's of similar buses with no sight of the sea in any direction that I looked. I recall the feelings of anxiety as I waited to get off the bus for I thought surely we must have come to the wrong place. (The coach park was actually about quarter of a mile from the sea front). When we finally arrived at the promenade the tide was out and I also recall that I kept asking; 'Where's the sea, where's the sea?' When pointed out, it appeared to me to be a thin grey line on the far horizon, and I was not really convinced until we walked across this vast, level expanse of sand, and finally to my great delight, there was the sea gently lapping toward us with small waves that began to break around my bare feet as we tentatively paddled out. We spent that glorious afternoon paddling and then collecting shells. Our meanderings led us about half a mile up the promenade from the clock tower on the main front. On the walk back down the prom a local photographer took a snap of Mum and Dad, also on the stroll back Dad gave me and our Bern a real treat when he bought both of us a peach at sixpence each. Up to that time we thought that all peaches came out of a tin and was served with condense milk. These large juicy yellow and reddish purple fruit, which we had never seen before in this form, tasted sensational and I sucked the large stone for about an hour afterwards.

Back in the town centre we had a fish and chip supper then me and our Bern sat on a wall outside a pub drinking bottles of lemonade whilst Mum and Dad when inside for a 'swift half of mild and bitter.' All too soon our sea side outing came to a close. It had been the most enjoyable day of my life and as soon has we boarded the bus I fell fast asleep. The summer holidays were nearly over and in September I was going to commence my primary school education at Gilbert Heathcote Junior Boys School on Whittington Moor.

At last that September Monday morning dawned when I stood in the school hall with lots of other poorly dressed boys waiting for some one to tell us what to do. As I gazed around my attention was drawn to a rather pathetic blonde haired figure who I knew had been crying as from his bright blue eyes tear streams had washed away the dirt on his face leaving white lines down his cheeks. His nose was running with the mucus forming 'candles' that seemed to run endlessly into his mouth. His jumper was thread bare and he appeared to have no socks, unless they had 'gone to bed.' He told me his name was John Gould from Duke Street. We would later always, with affection, call him Johnny. He was by no means unique in being poorly dressed as most of us were of similar attire, and was common practice; most of us did not adhere to the basic hygienic practice of wearing underpants. In fact the only boy that I can recall wearing underpants was Roger Huckerby.

A 'bullet' headed figure of a middle aged man whose intimidating look was exaggerated by having a completely bald head, ruddy complexion, and dressed in a grey three piece suit entered the hall accompanied by a group of adult people who turned out to be form teachers. The bullish man was the Headmaster, Eric Powell, known formally as E.R.L. Powell, a person who would have a great influence on my future career. Mr Powell opened the proceedings by giving us a 'pep' talk on expected behavioural and achievement standards with emphasis on the ethos of representing the school favourably to the adult population when outside the confines of school.

He then began a roll call of assigning kids to a particular form teacher and I was placed in Mrs Beresford's form 1A.

It wasn't so much that Mr Powell was intimidating it was rather that I held him in awe typified on one occasion as I was returning from a night out at the Hippodrome with my parents on the Friday night bus from Chesterfield to Newbold Moor seated on the lower, non smoking saloon deck. Mr and Mrs Powell were also passengers and I knew that they would alight before us at a stop on St Johns Road were they resided at 'Denewood.' Throughout the journey I was troubled by the thought that I would be recognised as they would have to pass by our seats. I was, and still do suffer from shyness and dreaded a face to face meeting with my Headmaster... Mr Powell, being the perfect gentleman acknowledged the family with a friendly comment and a brief glancing smile for me.

The Education Act of 1944 had just been implemented with its stated ethos that education not only has to do with communicating academic information but also should involve the whole person's academic abilities, spiritual, physical and vocational needs. Religion and spiritual values were of paramount importance by emphasis that every school day should begin with collective worship on the part of all pupils in attendance. The act also made it possible for a restricted number of pupils to gain free places in a Grammar School if they passed an examination at aged 11. This was generally known as the 11+ examination which tested the ability of children in two subjects only, namely, English and Arithmetic. Gilbert Heathcote School complied with the requirements of the education act, and with guide lines laid down by the LEA saw its main functions as imparting spiritual values and preparing its pupils for this particular examination.

Every school morning began with form registration and on three mornings, following registration, there was school assembly in the hall overseen by Mr Powell who began by leading the pupils in reciting ;'The Lords Prayer' followed by a short reading of scripture and closing with an hymn. Before dismissal Mr Powell would inspect all pupils' shoes for evidence of applied shoe polish. Many kids, which included me on occasions, had cardboard or newspaper inserts in their shoes to cover holes in worn out soles, and it was neigh on impossible to present clean tidy shoes at inspection. Offenders were publicly reprimanded and urged to 'do better.' Another humiliation was played out every Monday morning following registration when pupils requiring school meals, and who qualified for free school meals had to leave their form rooms to collect their weekly five dinner tickets from the school office. So much for the confidentiality promised to parents of pupils who qualified for, and then accepted free school meals. I myself did not qualify for free meals as my Dad was in regular employment and

I opted to go home for dinner. I do recall that every morning about eleven o'clock a van would arrive from the Central School kitchens and deliver the food in large stainless steel bins. Peter Wright who did have school 'dinner's' would often complain that the potatoes were chalky in texture and the cabbage was always wet, soggy, and had an awful smell. Asked about his pudding course it was generally 'frog's spawn,' meaning sago or semolina with a dollop of jam or 'spotted dick,' a suet pudding mixed with currants. I often heard boys, who had school meals, chanting a ditty about their meals that was something like this;

A-scab-a matter pudding and green snot pie,

Mixed together with a dead dogs eye,

Thickened up with a dose of camel shit,

All washed down with a cup of cold sick.

On the morning's that did not have assemblies and before classes began Mrs Beresford would walk around the classroom whilst reading to the class the *Tales of Brer Rabbit* from a huge book. If there was the slightest inattentive behaviour she would without any indication, or hesitation, swipe the book across the offenders head. The usual culprit, and often recipient was Gerald Hall who was strategically placed on the front row of desks by Mrs Beresford. I was more comfortably sat on the back row along side my friend Joey Buckerly.

At Edmund Street School in each year we were taught by one teacher and occupied the same classroom. Now at Gilbert Heathcote we had several teachers and rotated classes. Most of the teachers were middle aged as most of the younger teachers had been called up to serve in the armed forces. The exception was Miss Coulson who would later teach me Geography, I thought maybe she was about twenty four years old. The staff as I recall were; Senior Teacher, Mr

Hancock, affectionately called 'Daddy', Misses Sellars and Bort, Mrs Beresford, Messrs Holmes and Bingham. Later the staff was joined by an ex army PTI, Mr Reaney, who taught physical education and coached our excellent football teams. The caretaker was Danny Clarke who in his spare times raced greyhounds at Wheeldon Mill, a local unaffiliated 'flapping' track at the bottom of Station Road near Pottery Lane. For descriptions of the elaborate scams pulled at this particular greyhound track I highly recommend reading Len Thompson's 'Life Down T'Lane.'

I recall that 'Daddy' Hancock taught me elementary science and Mr Bingham teaching me arithmetic, both subjects which I found quite easy to comprehend. The sophisticated Miss Bort was my favourite teacher, not so much for her teaching of English more for her sheer presence in the class room. She always dressed in elegant satin two piece suits, usually in shades of purple or mauve, accessorised by black silk blouse with her long auburn hair coiffure in the latest Hollywood style. It was rumoured that Miss Bort and her twin sister, who was a pharmacist, had both been interned during the early part of the war as they were of German origin. It certainly added to their mystique and allure as I in my adolescent naivety imagined them has some sort of glamorous Mata Hari type espionage agents. Yes I had a huge crush on Miss Bort which was also shared by the majority of my class peer group. Miss Sellars, a rather frail personage, taught history, and as was fitting it was from the dawn of recorded time mainly concentrating on the hunter fisherman of the Stone and Bronze Ages. I recall one cold autumn morning were Miss Sellars was on duty in the play ground. As she blew her whistle to signify the end of the period of break and we then lined up for re-entry into the school building it was the first time I remember observing visible breath condensing in the cold air. At the same moment the breeze lifted the hem of her skirt revealing a coral pink under slip and black lisle stocking both of which had been extensively patched and darned. It crossed my mind that teachers must be very poorly paid.

As well as being our form teacher Mrs Beresford, in our first year, also taught us Geography and I well remember the lessons she gave us on 'the Dark Continent' i.e. Africa. I found these lessons most interesting and also was useful in identifying the geographic location of postage stamps from my collection on African Colony's such has Nyasaland, Tanganyika and Rhodesia. Most of these colonies no longer appear on modern maps. We did a topic on the Pygmies from the regions of Equatorial Africa and by coincidence Dad had salvaged from the cleansing department a model African native hut which I brought to school and Mrs Beresford kindly displayed it in the classroom. Of course, my natural egotism led me on to fashion a native figure from Harbutts plasticine, complete with tin foil loin cloth fashioned from a milk bottle top and armed with a matchstick spear and cardboard shield. Mrs Beresford made me 'ceremoniously' place the figure beside the hut, which caused me some embarrassment due to my shyness. Despite knowing the consequences of my actions I seemed to have self inflicted embarrassing situations on myself all through my life although some situations were not instigated by me, typical was the carry over conflict between me and a peer school pupil, Peter Cooper;

You may recall the incident with Peter in the playground at Edmund Street School when with no provocation he struck me in the face. This confrontation was to be repeated when we commenced our first year at Gilbert Heathcote, but with an entirely different outcome; During one playtime Dave Hodgson, a 'Billy Bunter' type character who ingratiating himself with the other kids by bribing them with .sweets he had stolen from his mothers sweet shop, sidled up to me 'Peter Cooper sess he can feit thee' he said. I though nothing of it until after lining up to go back to classes on Miss Sellars whistle command. I was made aware that Peter was standing behind me when he started to poke his finger in my back and chant 'One two three.' He would have continued with 'I'm the cock of thee and ever shall be.' But I didn't let him finish for I spun round and hit him full in the face, yes it was a 'right cowtailer,' that knocked him to the floor were he stayed down and started to cry. Miss Sellars having witnessed my action immediately told me to report to the Headmasters office. I timidly knocked on his office door and got a curt; 'Enter.' On my entry he half looked up and with a slight nod indicated that I should stand in front of his desk. 'Now lad, what have you done?' 'Please Sir I've been feitin' I replied in a tremulous tone of voice. 'Who else was involved?' 'Please Sir, Peter Cooper.' 'What class are you in?' 'Please Sir, Mrs Beresford's.' 'Wait there lad.' It was the first time that I'd been in his office, and stood there pondering my fate for what seemed an interminable time, for I knew as sure has God made little apples that I was going to get the stick. I stared straight ahead; fixing my gaze, on a glazed cabinet full of silver trophies behind the desk on the back wall hardly daring to move or draw breath. Mr Powell arrived back with Peter Cooper in tow. Being the sportsman that he had been, and was still actively involved with the administration of international athletics, Mr Powell gave me chance to explain my side of the story. 'Are you the same age?' he then asked, obvious to the fact that Peter towered over me. On affirmation he said 'Shake hands, and mean it.' Peter was the son of Aaron Cooper who farmed at Dunston Hole at the top of Dunston Road. After this fracas we became better acquainted and I actually visited the farm but again, unwittingly, I had enhanced my reputation as a tough fighter, which was entirely a false premise.

School fights usually evolved from third parties debating amongst themselves who could best who, and then try to broker a fight These kids either sought revenge for a previous beating or hoped to curry favour by flattery of prowess of their would be champion in order to gain acceptance and protection from him. If either of the two, or both 'prospects' were gullible enough to be swayed into a confrontation they found themselves surrounded by a circle of braying, bating kids goading them on to fight. I suppose much like an old cock fighting pit. This was the way Robert Troth and I came face to face in Gilbert Heathcote's playground at 4.00pm after school. I knew and respected Rob and his entire family. His Mum single handed, practically kept the school functioning with her cooking and cleaning. Fortunately for me Rob held the same regard for me and we soon came to the conclusion that we had each been misrepresented by what was said by third parties and amicably agreed that we would deprive these baying idiots of their sport.

Talking about sport, during my time at Gilbert Heathcote the school football teams were invincible. Sadly due to my infirmity I was never going to make any impression on Mr Reany, although when he first arrived and we played form football on the top field, he would often see that I had found space out on the left wing and would pass the ball to me. Each time I would be immediately caught in possession. He soon began to direct his passes elsewhere which were only to be expected. Nevertheless, I always enjoyed supporting with pride our school teams when they played at home on the top field. In the first two years the football team captain was Terry Woods who was imperious at centre half and we often won the majority of games. Later it was the mercurial Archie Smith, the son of my Dad's pal Bras who led out the team. I can see it all in my minds eye now of Archie running on to the pitch then kicking the ball high into the air, followed by the rest of the team, immaculately turned out in blue and white strip. Archie's ploy always seemed to demoralise the opposition and I believe it worked for in my last year the team went through the season unbeaten home and away. Maybe also their skill and consistent effort displayed by all members of the team may a have had something to do with their success.

The sloping playground at Gilbert Heathcote bordered the south side of the school buildings with the school entrance gate facing Sheffield Road. The length of the playground was nearly one hundred yards long and in winter the kids quickly compacted any snow fall into a glistening brown coloured ice slide. There could be as many as thirty kids at time travelling down the slide at incredible speeds. The more timid would go down in a chain linked together by holding each others hands, which in some cases proved to be more dangerous as the line would tend to create a whip like action that brought the line crashing down. Mr Powell's office faced directly on to the playground but he never banned any of the boisterous games or pastimes that he witnessed being carried out in the playground typically activities were British Bulldog and 'Dead Leg' were a sneak attack of kneeing someone on the thigh hard enough for the leg to go dead and cause the recipient to fall over.

Mr Powell had been a fine athlete who went on to adjudicate at the 1948 London Olympic Games and became President of the Three A's, the Amateur Athletic Association. I remember that the whole school were taken to the Odeon Cinema in 1948 to view a film of the London Games and Mr Powell was a prominent figure in quite a few scenes. The supporting feature film was the delightful story of the rise to international fame of the Harlem Globetrotters basket ball team. Talk about instant celebrity adulation from us kids who watched the likes of 'Goose' Tatum and 'Meadowlark' Lemon's dazzling ball handling and mesmerising dribbling skills. What an afternoon that was, but it did not escape my attention that it was really an exercise in instilling in our young minds the benefits of having mental and physical discipline as an escape route from our previous sub cultural backgrounds.

A more cultural ambitious outing was also arranged by the school; again the Odeon was the venue to view a film adaptation of Hamlet staring Laurence Olivier in the eponymous role. To me, at the age of 10 years old, it was quite beyond my comprehension and consequently a most boring exercise. I also sensed a gathering restlessness among my peers as I am sure they were having the same difficulty in comprehending the dramatic prose language of Shakespeare. This 'instant' culture offering was a complete waste of time on the majority of the kids that attended Gilbert Heathcote as there was no attempt at pre- preparation or later discussion on the subject matter. I suggest it was more appropriate to modern sixth form study.

In fact I had started to use the Chesterfield Children's Library as early as seven years old. Gilbert Heathcote did have a small collection of books housed in a locked, large wooden cupboard. The school 'library' monitor and key holder was Trevor Boyce, a senior pupil who made me well aware of my social background by the stigma of refusing to let me take any of the loan books home in case they would be vandalised. Therefore most Friday afternoon's after school a group of kids from Devonshire Street, including our Bern, Peter Wright and Roger Huckerby would walk the distance to and from the Chesterfield Library as we could not afford the two penny bus fare. I remember the first ever book that I borrowed was Dr Dolittle by Hugh Lofting which so fired my imagination that it inspired me to become a life long reader. Whilst at Gilbert Heathcote I read such stories as Charles Kingsley's Water Babies, R.M. Ballantyne's Coral Island, Captain Marryat's Masterman Ready, Rider Haggard's King Solomon's Mines and of course, Robert Louis Stevenson's Treasure Island. One of my favourite possessions at that time was a picture story book of Dickens's Oliver Twist that I obtained from a jumble sale.

I did try to read the Leatherstocking Tales of Fenimore Cooper after seeing the film '*The Last of the Mohicans*' starring Randolph Scott as Hawkeye at the Lyceum but Fenimore Cooper's nineteenth century style of grammar was to me, undecipherable. There was one passage however in his Last of the Mohicans, were Chingachgook is taking to Hawkeye, that I have always had a fondness for;

'Where are the blossoms of those summers!–fallen, one by one; so all of my family departed, each in his turn, to the land of spirits. I am on the hilltop and must go down into the valley; and when Uncas follows in my footsteps there will no longer be any of the blood of the Sagamores, for my boy is the last of the Mohicans.'

At about ten years old I discovered the science fiction Martian Tales series of books about John Carter War Lord of Mars by Edgar Rice Burroughs, better known as the author of the Tarzan series of books. As a ten year old I became besotted with one of the heroines Thuvia who was a Maid of Mars. In my adolescent years I had a tendency of 'falling deeply in love' with the heroine female fictional characters and remember having a heart yearning crush that lasted many months on Athenais, a French Aristocrats daughter who was the first love of author Dennis Wheatley's eponymous hero in *The Launching of Roger Brook*.

This popular reading matter was a far cry from the literature of William Shakespeare although I did in my early teenage years go on to read Erskine Caldwell's *Tobacco Road* and *God's Little Acre*, also John Steinbeck's *East of Eden* and *The Grapes of Wrath*. The last semi biographical novel that I read was Upton Sinclair's *The Flivver King* based on the rise of Henry Ford the founder of the Ford Motor Company and his brutal suppression of trade unions within his plants. After that I have tended only to read autobiographies.

There were two tragic events occurred whist I was at Gilbert Heathcote both relating to pupils in my own class which affected the whole school but members of our class in particular: Ronnie Evans a bright and effervescent young lad who lived on Racecourse Road just opposite Dadad's yard suffered from diabetes and of consequence had to administer insulin injections to himself on a daily basis. Ronnie never divulged his condition to class mates which I believed he perceived as a weakness that would undermine his natural 'gung ho' character. It was with utter shock that we were told by Mr Powell that Ronnie had died of causes relating to his diabetes problem. It was later elaborated on as a warning to other diabetes sufferers that Ronnie had, unbeknown to his parents or teachers had ceased taking his insulin injections and had quickly fallen into a deep coma from which he never recovered. One Monday morning we were told by Mrs Beresford that John Gould had died from drowning as a result of falling in the flood swollen River Rother whilst out playing with his brothers. This dreadful incident played on my mind for some considerable period of time. Even now I can vividly recall that awful morning. In them days there was no such thing as offering counselling to pupils.

Although I enjoyed attending Gilbert Heathcote for most of the time the lure of Dadad's yard would tempt me to occasionally play truant to spend time down there were when engaged on removing engine parts, or going out 'on business' with Jack or Sid, I had a sense of 'being grown up.' Some of these sojourns turned out to be embarrassing when our Jack, or Sid, would play a prank on me. Typical was one morning when we were travelling back to the yard along Sheffield Road our Jack turned into the school play ground and parked outside Mr Powell's office where he preceded to toot the car horn. I quickly scrambled into the back and tried to make myself invisible. To be fair to our Jack he immediately reversed the car then drove forward out of the play ground before anyone could investigate the noise. He actually thought it was funny!

Gilbert Heathcote School Championship Football Team 1948/49

Chapter 10 – Leonard Truman was Tarzan

He flies through the air

With the greatest of ease

That daring young man

On the flying Trapeze

OLD FOLK SONG

'Is Bernard in?' The question was posed to my Mum as she responded to a knock on our front door one Sunday morning in the summer of 1945, by a young man wearing a trilby hat, pulled down over his eyes, and dressed in a full length trench coat. Mum was taken aback by this rather sinister caller and whilst hesitating to answer the question our Bern came to the door and greeted this young man with; 'Hey up Len, come on in.' Turning to Mum our Bern said; 'Mum this Len Truman a pal of mine. I'm just going to show him our shed.' Len was sixteen years old and living with his Aunty and Uncle on Racecourse Mount and was currently employed at Sheepbridge Engineering as an apprentice fitter. He had just arrived in the West End and was introduced to our Bern by Keith Tasker who was a next door neighbour of Len's Uncle.

Len immediately made himself at home and sweet talked Mum into making him a dripping sandwich and cup of tea after which he offered her his profuse compliments. Obviously this went down very well with Mum and there after, he could do no wrong in Mums estimation.

At that time I was seven years old and our Bern was nine. It may seem to the reader, a rather odd friendship, considering the disparity in age between us and Len Truman, but our Bern had always gravitated to friendship with older boys and Len for his part, although possessing a keen mind coupled with a vivid imagination, was at that time immature for his age. He immediately became the natural leader of out group and I must say that he broadened our horizons in many, many respects during the eighteen months of our association before Len joined the Royal Navy.

Before Len came on the scene, we as a group, had often ventured as far a field as the Plantations that straddled Dunston Road then down through the Bull Fields to Walkers River with its backdrop of the 'Blue Tips,' a slag heap formed by waste from Nestfield Colliery, then into Kings Wood. That part of Walkers River that flowed from Cordwell Valley through Barlow then on down to the dams was pure and clean and supported trout, stickleback, minnows, bullyheads and crayfish with also an abundance of birdlife including kingfisher and dipper. Below the dam the river took on an ochre colour from deposits of iron oxide mined by Sheepbridge and smelted in coke ovens on the other side of the blue tips. When we swung across the river to gain access to the blue tips the water stained our feet a bright orange brown colour which was difficult to wash off. On the opposite side of Dunston Road from where now is located Duston Nurseries there stood a splendid Walnut Tree that every year was laden with nuts encased in green sheaths, which when removed left marks on your fingers identical to nicotine stains but with a more pungent aroma. We had a right palaver with Mum trying to convince her that we had not been smoking, as she, like most people, have never seen a walnut tree. I never knew who owned that tree, probably Dunstan Estates or The Duke of Devonshire, but sadly, many years ago it was cut down as the wood is a sought after and highly valued commodity. The wide open spaces of the Bull Fields were ideal for testing out our new bows and spears. It was no co-incidence that at senior school both me and Peter Wright threw the javelin and discus for our respective schools at the annual inter schools sports day held at the Queens Park. When Len took over leadership of the group we journeyed further afield covering the woodland right up to the village of Barlow including features such as the Sheepbridge Dams, the Lagoon, Monk Wood, and chiefly Cobnor Wood were Len had a secret hideaway which he called 'The Basin.' In actual fact it was a disused and overgrown sand stone quarry that was to be our base camp for the next three years;

I do not know how many hours Len worked at his fitting job for he seemed to spend all of his time at Sheepbridge in making for our group arrow and spear heads out of broken mechanical hacksaw blades which were a vast improvement on the old zinc that we had previously used. He also equipped all of us with an effective throwing knife, again ground from the broken blades. The handles were formed by black insulation tape which helped achieve a perfect balance that ensured the knife always landed point first. Now you may think that we were armed to the teeth and what was the purpose? As I have mentioned before we were influenced by the action adventure films that were characteristic of the film output of the 1940s, which we aped, especially Robin Hood, Westerns and most prominently Tarzan. We took great pleasure in shooting an arrow with a tempered steel point that buried itself into a tree. Or throw a spear that always landed point first. Yes, these simple activities gave us indescribable pleasure that can only be truly understood by other young kids who were also free to partake in similar activities. The only injuries we inflicted were to ourselves as I will later describe.

Len was the real hot shot with a bow. I recall one afternoon he had just entered Edie's back yard and was waiting for a game of cricket to end as we were all then going to Sheepbridge Dam for a swim. As usual he carried his bow with a quiver full of arrows strapped to his back. He stood facing the match with his back towards the boundary wall when the kid about to bowl shouted; 'There's a rat on wall.' Len whilst turning toward the wall notched an arrow drew back his bow then tracked the rat for an instant before loosing the arrow which pierced the rat's head. I have witnessed many feats of skill but none that measured up to that one.

We had been attending Stand Road swimming pool on a regular basis before meeting Len, but as yet, had not learned to swim. On our first foray to the Sheepbridge Dams with Len and his ever present border collie dog 'Paddy.' When we stripped Len without any warning threw Bernard into the water and when he surfaced Len immediately pulled him out and instantly threw him back in. On this occasion our Bern looked for assistance but Len told him to swim and amazingly he started to do a 'dog paddle stroke' and managed a few yards before Len help in out. Whilst all this was happening I kind of froze with fear only to be then addressed by Len who told me I had the option to dive in or like Bernard be thrown in. It was with great trepidation and uncontrollable body trembling that I stood on the water edge but could not move. Len gave me a gentle push and I found myself wallowing in murky yellow greenish water that tasted foul and smelled putrid. In an instant I was pulled out and was told by Len to run around the dam to keep warm. After a very short time had elapsed our Bern voluntary entered the water and managed a few strokes which made me envious and keen to try again. Within a week we were both swimming quite strongly and never looked back. I do not advocate this extreme method and I cannot quantify the danger of our possibility of drowning that we faced that day, but I somehow think Len knew exactly what he was doing and he saw no risk with this 'method in his madness.'

During the late forties the dams became our regular swimming venue were we would readily dive off the sluice valve wheelhouse, being careful not to swallow the water and in my case with eyes shut tight whilst under. We were still regular attendee's at Stand Road swimming pool but there was always crowds wanting access, especially on Saturdays and Sunday's when hourly session came into force. Mid week we could stay in the pool up to nine hours at a time for the admission price of two pence. We always swam naked at the dams, leaving our clothing in piles on the edge, and after our swim would then run around the dams until we were dry. On one occasion, after Len had left to join the Royal Navy, all the group were in the largest dam when quite surprisingly two teenage girls seemed to appear from nowhere and stood on the bank side daring us to come out. After some time past, it seemed like hours to me, they lost patience and in devilment scooped up the heaps of clothes and started on down the railway line towards Sheepbridge works and shouting back to us; 'You can't catch us.' We were in a right quandary as we did not have a stitch between us. The only cover that we could conceive was to wait until dark to make our way home, but being summer it would be a long wait. After what seemed an eternity the two girls, shouting a warning of their presence, returned our clothes.

They had the audacity to introduce themselves as sisters Jean and Mary Saint from Sheepbridge Square and explained that they had just done it for a 'giggle.' Co-incidentally, one of their elder brothers Ken would later marry my Aunty Ethel nee Ellis.

As previously mentioned the Basin in Cobnor Wood became our base camp and to that end we all built separate tree houses, in imitation of Johnny Weissmuller's Tarzan. The seven tree houses, two on one side, and five on the other side of the quarry had a connecting single rope swing fastened to a tall Sweet Chestnut tree that grew from the quarry floor. You could directly swing over to Len and our Bern's platform or perform a semicircular looping swing to get to someone on your side of the quarry. This amazing facility had been achieved by ingenuity, mainly on Len's part, and of course, trial and error. Typical was how to get the rope swing in the correct fastening position and more critical getting the exact rope length. Once again, our Bern psyche was questioned when it came to the task of sorting out the correct rope swing length. Len, using a hemp rope pilfered off a tarpaulin covered Sheepbridge railway wagon, made the initial swing trial but found it too short to reach across the quarry. He then asked our Bern to climb up the tree and lengthen the rope by about four foot. Our Bern duly carried the adjustment and shouted across to Len that he would stay up the tree in case the rope needed any further adjustment. Len commenced the second trial swing and just has he stared the upward motion the rope gave way and he fell some ten to twelve feet into some scrub on the quarry floor. Incredibly, apart from superficial scratching and bruising he had no injuries. What had really happened was that Bernard after making the adjustment then cut part way through the rope and when Len commenced his swing Bernard cut through the rest. When Len discovered what Bernard had done his only comment was; 'you daft bugger.' Bernard's laconic reply was; 'I thought it would be a laugh.'

To hone our craft skills sometimes we would divide into two groups and try to steal upon the opposing side and take them prisoner. At one such exercise Freddy Finney had decided to climb into a leafy tree and try to jump on either Len or our Bern as they passed under. He was sprawled across a lower branch and sure enough he espied our Bern creeping toward him in some long grass. Before Fred could jump down Bernard had spotted him and incredulously threw a knife up at Fred that pierced his right side. Fred fell from the tree and landed on his back which winded him for some seconds before he stood up and set off running in the direction of home. The wound turned out to be superficial and yet again Bernard's irresponsible behaviour did not get penalised. Bernard's actions were not always turned outwards as at one particular time we had been scrumping apples from Davis's orchard, which was situated were Fisher's Lane met Duston Lane, and on the way home he would persist in throwing an apple in the air then try to slice it with a knife. On one try he let go of the knife which stuck in his shin. He hobbled home with the knife still intact. In our kitchen we cleaned the wound with dettol and affixed a plaster which had to suffice as we dare not tell Mum what he had done.

Border collie dogs are known for their intelligence and Len's dog Paddy was no exception. He was a well trained and very obedient animal who was a constant companion to Len and a great delight to us kids as he entertained us with his many tricks. Len had brought an extra dimension to our childhood and I have very fond memories of that special eighteen months before Len's departure. It was with great regret to me that some months later Len would die as a result of a motorcycle accident at his naval base in Devonport.

For the next couple of years we would frequently visit the haunts that Len had introduced us to and will now describe a typical incident that typifies our privileged childhood that was the freedom to roam at will through the area known as Sheepbridge woods; On our way to visit the dam for a swim we detoured to watch some baby rabbits that had a burrow on the top of the blue tips. There was a railway siding on the far side of the tip were we espied a wagon with a brand new green tarpaulin cover. Having 'removed' the tarpaulin for our own use we decided to make our way to a swampy area of water that we called the 'lagoon'. I think it was used as a settling overspill pool to the dams that were located in the same vicinity. The idea was to build a canoe using the canvas and willow wood framework. On completion it was found to be very unstable and had tendency to 'turn turtle.' Being familiar with South Sea Island films usually starring Jon Hall and Maria Montez which featured 'outrigger' canoes we decided to incorporate such a feature on our canoe. It looked to have solved the problem of stability and so Roger Huckerby volunteered to try it out and squeezed into the space between the two rigger support spars. As Roger paddled out the canoe floated for several minutes then the canvas, which was not waterproof, began to leak water to the inside of the canoe. Rog trying to get out found that he could not extricate himself from the two cross spars and was slowly sinking with the craft. The water was only about two feet deep but being swamp, beneath the water was a morass of sludge that precluded wading out to the stricken canoe and the floundering Roger. The swamp was surrounded by willow trees but they were too flimsy to take anyone's weight. I don't know who thought of it but it was decided to cut down several willow 'wands' and tie them together using our socks. Using this extended line we were able to float it out and then pull Roger to safety.

Before closing this chapter I will relate one more escapade that we participated in during the summer of 1946. Whilst following the railway line that skirted the edge of Monk Wood on its way to Barlow we discovered a shale outcrop that was part way full of murky water which had a 'rainbow' oil film on its surface. The water was maybe twenty feet deep and we would take sheer delight in jumping into this water from a height of about the same as the water's depth. The water was always freezing cold and stank of 'coal tar' and when emerging our skin was covered with this film. Yes it was extremely foolhardy and dangerous, but this aspect never entered our childish psyche. Paraphrasing a line from a Paul Newman biographical film on the life of the boxer Rocky Graziano; 'Somebody up there likes us.'

Roger Huckerby age 11

Chapter 11 – Any Old Iron

The only way to get rid of

Temptation is to yield to it.

OSCAR WILDE

The winter of 1947 was one of the most prolonged and coldest on record. It persisted from mid January to mid March with snow, and freezing temperatures dropping as low as minus twenty degrees. My outstanding memory of that time was of seeing gigantic icicles suspended from every roof guttering and reaching well below bedroom window sills. My memories always go back to those freezing conditions when I hear these lines spoken from Shakespeare's 'Love's Labour's Lost;'

When icicles hang by the wall

And Dick the shepherd blows his nail

And Tom bears logs into the hall

And milk comes frozen home in pail.

Fuel such as coal, already in short supply due to post-war shortages, was difficult to get due to the weather. Even when supplies were available it was sometimes impossible to get a delivery because of the huge snow drifts that impeded the distribution by horse and cart. This period was the first time I can recall that school actually had to close for short periods for lack of heating fuel. We kids thought this was great and spent this time sledging down Devonshire Street.

By the summer of 1947 we, the Devonshire Street group, had been going to the open air swimming pool at Stand Road for some considerable time. During spring and autumn school terms we would normally go to the 8pm till 9pm session, and at the weekends, were due to demand, hourly swimming sessions at a cost of three pence, would come into force. Sometimes if we had no money we would go up to the Sheepbridge dams for a swim. During the long summer holiday weekdays, if there were no evening clubs booked, you could sometimes stay in the pool from 10am to 9pm, for one admission cost, which we often did.

About 8pm on the August evenings Arthur Lucas, the pool superintendent would turn on the two floodlights and it was most exhilarating to 'torpedo' jump out of the darkness of the twenty foot high diving board into the eight foot deep end of the lit pool trying to plunge through a floating lorry rubber inner tube.

Sunday mornings during the high summer months the pool became a meeting place of social discourse and recreation for juvenile, teenage and young adult persons. By 10am there would be forming a queue of maybe one hundred persons waiting for the first session to commence. Many of the older patronage were affluent enough to arrive on touring bicycles which were leaned against the outside wall and left unattended for the whole of the hourly swimming session. Our Bern had taught me how to ride using his old Rudge bicycle but it was frustrating to me not owning one of my own, hence one Sunday morning I commit a rather stupid act of stealing one of the parked bicycles at the swimming pool. The adult bicycle's frame was too large for me to sit on the saddle and reach the pedals but I managed to ride it home sitting on the cross bar and weaving side to side. Devonshire Street was only a ten minute walk from Stand Road so the bike journey was done in a few minutes. On arrival my Mum went 'ballistic' and to frighten me said that the police would be here at any minute if I did not immediately return the bike, which I did without anyone else being the wiser. Mum did not tell Dad or our Bernard, and instead of being punished, she persuaded Dad to buy our Bern a second hand Raleigh off Wilf Sims for his eleventh birthday in July. I then became the proud owner of the multi-coloured Rudge.

The lads from the West End would congregate with their bikes on the bottom outside Jackie Tucker's shop and show off by doing 'wheelies' or racing around a makeshift dirt track on the waste ground along side the tin mission. I recall one afternoon when Louis Sims, we called him Loy's, reared his bike up to do a wheelie and the front wheel dropped out of its forks. He struggled to get the bike under balance control but in so doing ran into a gas lamp and knocked out his two front teeth. Of course, everybody laughed at his antics and gave no assistance with his facial injury.

Talking about bike incidents Monk Sims, Louis's younger brother, supplied me with a set of rubber brake blocks to replace the worn out ones on my bike front braked wheel. As part of the deal Monk also agreed to fit them as the Rudge had a two part, steel actuating brake rod that needed adjusting by a grub screw fastening arrangement using a special Allen Key tool that was in Monk's possession. With replacement brake blocks fitted I set off on my bike from the Sims house on Racecourse Mount and turned down Devonshire Street. As I began the descent I applied the brake and to my consternation only the top part of lever moved, leaving the bottom rod that was attached to the pads motionless. Monk after making the adjustment had not tightened the grub screw sufficiently, leaving me without a brake. I tried to put my feet to the ground, the action of which only served to jar my ankles. I thought that if I could make the bottom right hand turn safely on to lower Mountcastle Street I would be able to coast to a halt. Gritting my teeth and gulping for breath I leaned the bike over and at break neck speed navigated the turn only to be confronted by a nightmare situation for parked outside Jack Slight's shop was an Andrews Ice Cream Van and crossing the road toward it four small girls. People often tell me that in that sort of situation the action appears to slow down and your whole life passes before you. I don't know about my life but I do recall that I certainly seemed to have time to consider my limited options of either crashing into the van or knocking down the kids. There was in fact no real choice, for I steered straight for the van, which fortunately for me had all its shutters open. It really was like a scene out of a silent movie comedy as on contact I took a header into the van interior, sliding across the ice tub and colliding with the vendor. I remember to this day his very words to me were;' Come in kid, make thee sen at hom.' I was that embarrassed I pretended to have been knocked unconscious.

Someone must have recognised me for within minutes I could hear my Mum's hysterical shouting and with a peeping glimpse I was aware that our immediate neighbour, Joe Hall, was carrying me up Devonshire Street. Joe set me down on our settee and said he would try to contact a doctor, all this time Mums hysterics never ceased. After Joe left I said;'Oh shut up Mum, I'm alright.' 'I was only pretending.' When Dr. Dornan arrived Mum had dutifully covered me with a blanket and was administering aspro tablets dissolved in warm water. For she was now ashamed at calling out Dr.Dornan under false pretences for the only casualty was the bike that suffered a buckled front wheel and broken chain. After Dr.Dornan left, having first given me a check up and was satisfied that I was comfortable, Mum immediately despatched me to bed as a punishment. I thought that this was most unfair as the incident had not been my fault and all of my remonstrations fell on deaf ears meaning that I was condemned to miss an episode of 'Dick Barton' on the radio.

When the BBC light programme came on the air in 1946 it ushered in a 'golden age' of radio light entertainment, featuring music, drama and comedy and for the following seven years it provided high quality programmes that appealed to the mass population, which held sway until Coronation year 1953, when television sales really took off and eclipsed the radio. Typical programmes from 1946 and 1947 to which I was an avid listener were; *Dick Barton, Special Agent – The Adventures of PC 49 – Have a Go – Two-Way Family Favourites – Much Binding in the Marsh, Up the Pole* and *Paul Temple*.

Weekdays at 6.45pm, just after the news the streets would become deserted as 15 million listeners tuned into the BBC light programme to hear the introductory theme music 'Devil's Gallop' that preceded then heralded the announcer Hamilton Humphries rap out 'Dick Barton... Special Agent!' I cannot recall any other broadcast that had this mass adulation until the television era when 'Hancock's Half-Hour' and 'The Kenny Everett Show' would empty public houses. The fifteen minute long episodes of Dick Barton were full of fast paced tongue-in-cheek adventures as Dick and his two sidekicks Snowey and Jock usually found themselves in some pretty tight spots from which they always managed to extricate themselves. The cliff-hanger ending were always emphasised by Hamilton Humphries dramatic voice over the closing theme tune typically rapping out; 'What is the secret of the room?' 'What happened to the man who screamed?' What is crawling toward Dick, Snowey and Jock?' The theme tune then increases in volume and after a short pause Humphries closes with 'Listen to the next instalment of Dick Barton... Special Agent.

The Adventures of PC 49 was a fore runner of the TV series 'Dixon of Dock Green,' both being about ordinary Bobbies on the beat solving crimes in fictional Divisions of the Metropolitan Police. But that is were the similarities ended for Jack Warner as an aging PC George Dixon with his introductory catch phrase 'Good Evening All' and benevolent cosy father figure portraying an ordinary copper with phrases such as 'chummy' and 'having your collar felt' and no matter what the nature the crime he had solved, always ending each episode with reassuring words to the effect that 'Crime does not pay.' Whereas, the younger Brian Reece as 'PC 49' (Police Constable Archibald Berkeley-Willoughby) portrayed a whimsical, public school accented plodding character who's catch phrase was 'Oh, my Sunday helmet!' who despite always playing down his brilliant crime solving abilities to his superior Detective Inspector Wilson (played by Leslie Perrins) in every episode, but to his consternation, was always championed by his posh spoken girl friend Joan played by the popular singing star Joy Shelton. Every episode ended by DI Wilson saying; 'Out you go 49.'

'Have a Go' was an outside broadcast programme presented by Wilfred Pickles. Its wide general appeal was because it was a celebration of ordinary folk who were encouraged to tell heart-warming stories and share experiences of their families. If he had a young contestant he would say in his thick Yorkshire accent; 'Are yer courtin.' Afterwards they were invited to Have a Go and answer four simple quiz questions with Wilfred helping them along making sure that every contestant won the prize money of £1.18s 6d. At which stage he would call out his catchphrase 'Give 'em the money, Barney!' with reference to Barney Colehan the show producer. Later Barney was replaced by Wilfred's wife 'Mabel at the table. The resident piano accompanist was Violet Carson later to gain immortality as the character Ena Sharples in Coronation Street.

'The time in Britain is twelve noon, in Germany its one o'clock, but home and away it's time for Two-Way Family Favourites' an announcement familiar to an audience of more than 12 million as they sat down to Sunday lunch and listen to Jean Metcalfe in London and Cliff Michelmore in Hamburg exchange greetings from families at home to their beloved ones serving with the BAOR (British Army of the Rhine) and play a requested song from gramophone records. Jean and Cliff fostered such an agreeable partnership, that was most evident to the listeners, that they eventually married in 1950. Cliff went on to be the main presenter of the TV current affairs programme 'Tonight' I remember Cliff during a live Tonight transmission having a two-way discussion with the female presenter Polly Elwhis who was interviewing children during a nature lesson in a Junior School. One little boy was holding up a privet branch and Polly informed Cliff that it contained a Stick Insect. Obviously Polly had never seen a Stick Insect for as she peered ever closely at the branch the camouflaged green coloured four inch long insect brushed past her nose.

Down went the microphone and with a piercing shriek of terror Polly disappeared off the screen. Polly later married in 1960, the BBC sports presenter Peter Dimmock.

The cult comedy programme *Much Binding in the March*, set in a fictitious backwater RAF station whose inmates were forever finding ways to circumvent the constraints of ministry red tape, starred Kenneth Horne, Richard Murdock and Sam Costa. The dialogue and jokes relied heavily on topical events, as with many 40's and 50's radio comedy, and would make little sense to the modern listener. This series of programmes along with Tommy Handley's ITMA laid the 'blueprint for many other comedy series such as 'Round the Horne and Take it from Here.'

Up the Pole featured the comedy double act of Jimmy Jewel and Ben Warriss. The pair was cast as cross-talking proprietors of an Artic trading post and ran on radio until 1951. It was pure Max Wall type musical hall patter and made them the highest paid double act of the early 1950s.

From 1946 to 1951 Kim Peacock as Paul Temple and Marjorie Westbury as his wife Steve held the listeners transfixed with excitement tempered with fear as week by week they acted out the 'who dunnit' plots devised by the creator of the series Francis Durbridge. The two outstanding series that I can recall were 'The Gregory Affair, 'and the very frightening and sinister 'The Sullivan Mystery.' Every series ended with Paul Temple throwing a party at which the criminal perpetrator would eventually be unmasked despite Steve's pre-meddling actions that put Paul in mortal danger of his life. Because Mr Thompson our life insurance man always surprised us with his devised surprise appearances at our front door Mum always whispered 'Shush, Its Kim Peacock.'

One early Monday morning in mid August 1947 I stood excitedly, but also impatiently with bucket in hand in Devonshire Street along side other kids, including our Bern, waiting for Dan Haslam's tractor and trailer to arrive to take us to his farm at Cutthorpe to commence a period of potato picking. During the bumpy twenty minute journey up Dunston Road to the potato fields we would noisily talk of how we were going to spend our earnings, and would take a swig from a shared bottle of water that formed part of our packed lunch of potted meat sandwiches. Starting at 8.00am and finishing around 6.00pm was a long and arduous day especially during a short spell of very hot weather. Our task was to walk along the freshly turned furrows and fill our bucket with the exposed potatoes which were then taken to a waiting trailer for transportation to a storage barn. I remember on that first day the terrible back ache I suffered from the constant bending and stretching but as the days wore on I got used to it and it did me no harm. The potato picking season lasted about ten days for which each of us were paid at a rate of 1s per day. Adults were paid slightly more at 1s.6d. Bernard and I got to keep 5s each from our earnings and part of this was used to refurbish our bikes.

Another opportunity to earn a small amount of money each year was in blackberry picking.

Sunday afternoons throughout late August and September we would visit a secluded area located about half a mile to the rear of Sheepbridge A and B Blocks which we called 'Stormy Hollow' that was overgrown with blackberry bramble bushes. It would take about three to four hours for two of us to fill a shopping size basket of ripe berries which we would sell to locals around the West End for 1s. Gathering blackberries was very labour intensive and demand far out stripped our supply capacity. Alas, Stormy Hollow is no more as it was part of the area allocated for the A61 Dronfield Bypass built in the early 1980s. There are still a few bramble bushes by the side of the bridle path that flanks the A61 but nothing like the profusion that once flourished there. Again most of our earning was spent on our bikes.

With money in our pockets we would visit Wards Cycle Shop situated on the corner of Sheffield Road and Avenue Road to peruse their comprehensive stock of spares, tools and accessories on the lookout for anything that would 'enhance' the appearance of our bikes. They had a huge collection of multi coloured dry transfers ranging from small at 1d to ones over a foot long at 3p each. Their motifs were designed as eye catchers such as 'Red Dragon' and 'Ace of Spades' that certainly appealed our adolescent intellect. They were so cheap that we would ring the changes every week. De rigueur were a John Bull puncture repair kit, water bottle and saddle bag along with handlebar tape, box spanner, all-in-one oil and Japanese lacquer paint. Our Bern's Raleigh originally had straight handlebars which he replaced by racing drop handle bars. The straight bars were fitted to my Rudge in place of the 'sit up' type bars that were more conventional.

We had bought an old OS map of Derbyshire from a jumble sale and each Saturday night after coming back from the first house of the Lyceum the Devonshire group would meet up in our yard and plan a cycle ride route for the following day. Typical routes were Matlock, Bakewell, Bamford and Castleton. After the planning the bikes were inspected and oiled and sometimes repainted or redecorated with new transfers. Most of our routes took us through Cutthorpe over Eastmoor then down to the Robin Hood public house were, just before entering the village of Baslow; we would take our first break for a drink of water at the Robin Hood cave on Chesterfield Road. As we sat on the roadside we would look with envy at the numerous cycle clubs that came flowing past us with each member astride a modern light weight touring cycle that in those days cost about £12.00, that represented what Dad earned in three weeks.

Freddy Jones who lived opposite us on Devonshire Street managed to beg an ex scout cotton canvas six berth ridge tent, and during the spring of 1948 most weekends it was usually pitched in the field at the back of our house. Although it was only supposed to be a six berth up to twenty kids would crowd into it which generated stifling hot conditions and if it rained and someone inadvertently touched the tent side it would immediately let in water as the proofing had long since ceased to be effective. Freddy and Ronnie Huckerby who also owned a small two berth ridge tent were planning to camp out in a farmer's field at Freebirch on Eastmoor for a week during the Summer holidays and asked if anyone else would be interested in going. We immediately sign up and started to squirrel away tins of food to take with us. By early July there must have been over a dozen kids eager to participate in this first ever camping experience. Our Bern didn't fancy the prospect of the overcrowded conditions and good chance of getting wet through in Freddy's tent due to the ever increasing numbers and asked Dad if he could have a tent from Wakefield's Army Stores for his birthday. Surprisingly, Dad agreed and we became the proud posses of a brand new 'Gale Force Two' olive drab canvas ridge tent with built in ground sheet, that could easily be transported strapped to a bike saddle. We tried it out by pitching it in the back field and were as you say; 'Snug as a bug in a rug.' With a couple of days to go before we were due to set off to Freebirch Dad for some still unexplained reason forbade us to go. So on the great day we forlornly saw the group off and as a small recompense Dad suggested that we could erect the tent in our bedroom that night and would be allowed to sleep in it, which we did. It was late July and it was one of those warm, clammy nights were you want to kick off the bed coverings to keep cool. Instead we were tucked up in sleeping bags inside the tent and after a very short time due to the humidity we were suffering from hyperventilation. We were drenched in sweat but managed to extricate ourselves from the sleeping bags and crawl out of the tent. I dread to think what may have happened if we had actually fallen asleep.

The last time I rode the old Rudge It was one Saturday afternoon in 1949 and I was stranded at the top of Grange Hill at Oxton Rakes trying to repair an inner tube that consisted mainly of patches and weakness 'blebs'. Every time I tried to inflate the tube it would burst in another area. By pure co-incidence our Jack was passing in a car and stopped to give me a lift back to the yard with the bike precariously balanced in the open boot. It had also been a bad day for our Jack as he had wasted his time going to Hathersage to collect owing money off the local Police Constable who was absent from his address. I never knew our Jack to swear or lose his temper but when we arrived back at the yard he started to rant and rage about Dadad' having a soft time of it' being at a football match at Saltergate with his pal Bill Madin while he had to chase up debts and run the yard single handed. Our Sid had just gotten married and was having a weekend at Skegness. Our Jack had every reason to feel aggrieved has he worked seven days a week at the yard and Dadad kept him and our Sid on bare basic wages. In addition to working all day at the yard they took turns six evenings a week to ferry Dadad to and from the Victoria Club on Sheffield Road. When our Jack finally calmed down and closed the yard at 4pm he said 'Come on Bry, I'll take you up Devo.' Instead of going up Racecourse Road our Jack went across Sheffield Road and parked at Ward's shop where to my complete surprise he exchanged the Rudge for a second hand refurbished BSA drop handle bar touring cycle. I was over the moon with excitement but couldn't bring myself to ask him what it had cost and he never mentioned it.

Our Jack was always of a generous nature but sometimes the gifts were not always solicited or even wanted. He would turn up unexpectedly at our house at dinner time with a pet of some kind in tow, usually taken in part exchange for a motor spare part. After having a bit of dinner and a cup of tea he would take his leave and on parting would say; 'Oh Hilda, can you look after this for a couple of days?' That's how all of our pets came to us, as he never asked for them back.

In the spring of 1958 I met Barbara, my future wife. We had been going steady for about two months when on a Friday evening we had been to the Regal Cinema to see Tommy Steele in. 'The Duke Wore Jeans,' and although she was nineteen at that time she was expected, by her father, to arrive back home by 10pm so we were waiting for the 9pm bus to Old Whittington when a car pulled to the kerb side. The occupants were our Jack and his wife Nora. Jack shouted; 'Get in I'll run you home.' As we passed the Royal Hospital instead of taking the right fork to Whittington Moor our Jack veered left heading for Newbold. I quickly reminded him that Barbara lived at Old Whittington to which he replied;

'We'll just call for a quick drink before I drop you off.' We ended up at the Rutland Arms Inn at Baslow where we stayed till 3am. Every protestation was met with; 'We'll just have another.' When we finally reached Barbara's home in the early hours her father who was stood at the front gate frantic with worry turned me away uttering words something like; 'If you want to live don't ever call for my daughter again,' I though in the circumstance he had let me off lightly for I was expecting to be man handled. I turned up outside their house for two weeks but did not catch sight of Barbara until one evening her sister Pat was drawing the front bedroom curtains and on seeing me and by way of excuse asked her Dad if Barbara could nip out to fetch her and her infant daughter some fish and chips. The rest was our future history and the subject of a second book.

Our Jack could be a saint, but sometimes he was the very devil.

Chapter 12 – Penny Doon, Penny Doon

In all things of nature there

Is something of the marvellous

ARISTOTLE

As the Whitsun excursion train from Chesterfield via Sheffield Victoria to Belle Vue Manchester pulled up to wait for the home signal on the outskirts of Gorton (Belle Vue) Station there appeared on the line side dozens of ragamuffin kids shouting up at us, the passengers, for 'Penny Doon, Penny Doon. I was used to seeing kids from poor areas like the West End but this poverty was even more striking by their emaciated gaunt frames, filthy ragged clothing and wild animal like actions as they fought with each other for the few pennies that were tossed from the carriage. That was the abiding memory of that Monday in 1948 when our family was having a day out at the world famous Belle Vue Zoological Gardens and Fairground in Manchester.

In the early morning the steam train pulled slowly in to Chesterfield Midland Station and we all piled into a compartment of a non-corridor coach. I was impressed by the big plush bench seats upholstered in green and brown moquet with white cotton anti stain head cloths embodied with the railway motif above which were overhead storage racks of cord netting. There was even a dome shaped electric light in the roof. Above one of the doors was an emergency communication cord that had an instruction 'Pull cord to stop the train. Misuse penalty £10. 'Of course our Bern was dying to test this out but on dissuasion by Dad he then turned is attention to the door window strap. The strap had holes in it just like a belt and these engaged with a brass pin on the door. The railway porter had closed the door with its window shut but in no time Bernard had sussed how to open it by disengaging the leather belt from the pin which to his consternation whipped out of his hand and flew past his chest due to the weight of the window. Nonplussed, he kept fiddling with the belt by engaging different holes with the stud and switching the light on and off. Our coach was near the rear of the train and on each curve our Bern would poke his head out of the open window to see if he could see the engine.

Never ever having been on this line before we were caught quite unaware as the train entered the three mile long Woodhead tunnel and smoke and steam began pouring in through the compartment open window filling it with a hot acrid atmosphere that smelled like burnt cinders making breathing difficult and eyes smarting from a stinging pain. In the dark it took Dad some time to find the light switch and then eventually close the window. The dimly lit acrid atmosphere inside the compartment only emphasised the complete blackness outside and it seemed an interminable, and to me, a very apprehensive time before we came out of the other end of the tunnel into the welcoming daylight. On arrival at Belle Vue Station we all had to have a tuppeny 'wash and brush up' to rid us of a sooty compound smeared across our faces and hands but the acrid burnt cider smell which had clung to our clothes and hair still lingered most of the day.

The zoological park had a pungent smell that reminded me of rotting or decaying compost which was intensified by the heat of the day. The odour was ever present as we strolled round the park staring at an assortment of listless animals in their caged enclosures. It struck me that the only natural animal activity was taking place high up in the Gibbon caged enclosure were these lesser-apes antics of travelling at high speed from bar to bar and leaping great distances with one jump attracted a large crowd.

There were two other attempts at providing a 'natural' environment, one was the penguin pool with its waterfall and spiral concrete walkway, which the inmates seemed to enjoy, and the other was the open air Hippopotamus pool surrounded by a circular four foot high concrete wall. We had to be given a 'leg up' by Dad to get a glimpse of the hippo's. As we began to leave this area our Bern decided that he would like a closer look at the hippo's and un-noticed by the rest of us slipped back and climbed on top of the enclosure wall and taking up a kneeling position was leaning into the pool area very close to a large hippo that had an enormous jaw spread revealing huge tusk like teeth. His antics, and the commotion it caused, drew Dads attention and he quickly turned back and 'yanked' our Bern off the wall. Now I believe that hippo's are vegetarian but this one could easily have taken our Bern into its cavernous jaws and given him a right mauling. Mum was hysterical and sobbing uncontrollably from the experience and Dad was so angry he took Bernard by the arms and was shaking the life out of him whilst also reprimanding him. Bernard's reaction was a look of incomprehensive disbelief that he warranted this reaction and treatment by his parents for what he perceived as natural inquisitiveness.

Our planned 'wonderful' day out had, to this point, been a catalogue of one minor mishap after another and by mid afternoon we were all feeling rather tired and dispirited which was not made any better by the exorbitant charge of 1s.3d each for a dried out corned beef sandwich and lukewarm cup of weak tea. As we sat there pondering how we would occupy our time until it was time to board the train at 7pm, a rather strange looking family walk by. This family of two parents and a small girl and boy attracted the attention of everyone sitting in the paved café area as there foreign appearance and mode of dress of brightly coloured tunics was so very different from the rather drab post war garb we were used to. They had already attracted a small crowd following up behind them and were certainly more interesting to us than any of the animal exhibits on show. To my now utter shame I must confess that we actually joined the crowd and followed this family for some few minutes. To their credit they kept a dignified if somewhat aloof indifference to the ever growing crowd of gawping onlookers. This was a time when there was no mass immigration of foreign nationals into Great Britain and we in our small parochial world had only mixed with white Europeans. This family group I found out were oriental Chinese.

After our session of 'people watching' Bernard and I badgered Dad and Mum to visit the Funfair section which was dominated by a huge blue and white painted wooden undulating structure with at its topmost curvature there was a huge white sign with the word BOBS displayed in red. I believe at that time this was the largest roller coaster in Europe and frightened the living daylights out of me. There were also two smaller, but still intimidating structures as I recall; one was the Scenic Railway and the other a fear some roller coaster with a car shaped like a mouse. We did persuade Dad to part with the fare to have a ride on The Caterpillar an undulating chain of cars that steadily speeded up and then a green canvas canopy swung over the cars. Again this part of the amusement park looked really rundown and smelled of hot grease and exhaust fumes.

It had been a very tiring day and I in particular was glad to board the train, and fortunately the journey back home was in the darkness of the evening light and I was only aware of re-entering the Woodhead tunnel by the slight whooshing noise that affected the rhythmic 'dadadada, dadadada' of the train wheels passing over the rail joints. As I was gently hushed to sleep by the gentle sway of the train and the rhythmic chant of the wheels little did I realise that in the space of three short years I would be again viewing the BOBS but from a specific viewpoint that would point the way to my future career as a mechanical design engineer and teacher.

Chapter 13 – There It Was, Gone

Into my heart an air that kills

From yon far country blows

What are those blue remembered hills

What spires, what farms are those?

This is the land of lost content

I see it shining plain

The happy highways where I went

And cannot come again

A.E.HOUSMAN

A Shropshire Lad

In the spring of 1948 a number of the residents of Devonshire Street gathered at the top of the street and looked on with bemused amazement as a gang of workmen demolished the imposing courtyard properties belonging to the Bunting and Barge families. To the onlookers it did not seem to make sense, as architecturally and structurally they were far superior to the terrace housing, they themselves, occupied. Other than the enormous dust clouds created I sadly remember the destruction of numerous house sparrow and starling nests with their chicks and eggs crushed by the falling debris. It later transpired that this demolition was in order to clear an access from Racecourse Mount to the meadow land behind Devonshire Street which had been acquired by The Chesterfield Borough Council as a site for development of a vast council housing estate spreading as far as Dunston Lane.

In what seemed no time at all Racecourse Mount was extended into the new infrastructure of Kendall Road that linked to Dunston Lane. The new Leavens Way was then built from St John's Road to intersect Kendall Road, and Lancaster Road was also extended to intersect with Kendall Road. More immediate to us was the digging of a trench for a mains sewerage drain that located just over our boundary wall. The trench ran from the new Kendall Road infrastructure down to Riddings Brook were further development would create Coniston Road. The trench excavation required heavy plant including an excavator, bull dozer, scraper and dump truck. I recall the dump truck driver in particular as a rather 'jack the lad' type character who became rather friendly with Mum as she was the first resident to offer to fill his mashing can with tea.

The drains trench ran through a heavy clay soil which gave off a distinctive fresh odour that I became addictive to, and I would spend many hours sat on our wall chatting to the gang of men busily engaged with laying the large diameter concrete sewer pipe sections. At that time it did not really dawn on me that this was the beginning of the end of our playground that would in the short space of eighteen months disappear forever under the bricks and mortar that was to become the sprawling Dunston and Newbold Moor estate. And by the mid seventies further development would even engulf the old West End that I had known and is no more. Indeed; 'There it was, gone.'

The ongoing building of Levens Way did provide our gang with a 'new' adventure playground were during weekends when the builders did not work we would explore the bare brick structures and climb up to the scaffoldings and jump from house to house. Again there were distinctive smells of newly planed deal, new plaster and fresh paint. We would get covered in cement dust which seeped into every pore. The workmen always left there mashing cans on site and we would use them when making oxo. I cannot recall who of our gang came up with the suggestion that we should 'as a point of honour' make sure that we defecated under the down stair floorboards of every house, which of course we did.

When the Coniston Road house building phase commenced Charlie 'Wag' Mellors from Devonshire Street acquired the post as night watchman and was allocated a small wooden shed as base. It was very snug inside having a pot bellied stove, small table, and easy chair. One Sunday afternoon Bernard, Roger Huckerby and I had been searching the building site for any scraps of 'brattice' cloth, a tarred cloth used as a waterproof roof lining, that we could use to cover the roof of our newly built rabbit hutch. We had just located an end of roll piece about three feet long that had been discarded near the watchman's shed, and noticed that Charlie was inside 'brewing up.' Just as an act of pure devilment we slipped a batten of wood through the wooden 'D' door handle to stop Charlie exiting, and then we tapped on the window. Charlie was going berserk as he rattled the flimsy ledge and brace door but the batten held firm. For some unfathomable reason, Roger then climbed upon the roof and urinated down the smoke stack, then covered the stack with his coat which he sat on. We could actually see the clouds of steam issuing from the stove as Roger jumped off the roof, and we then made a quick departure leaving the door fastened. We thought no more about it until about mid week when a police constable came knocking on our door with a summons for our Bernard to appear at the Juvenile Court charged with stealing 'a roll' of brattice cloth.

We had in the previous months been a bane to Charlie as we lead him a merry dance whilst trespassing on the building site. We would also lay in wait for him to come down the field passing by our back wall where we pretend to shoot at him using an unloaded toy 'pop' gun that actually fired corks, but I would instead, lob small stones at him. This latter action was, if you pardon the pun, to misfire on our Bern at his hearing.

Prior to the court appearance Mum and Bernard had met up with a member of the probation service who had explained the procedure and advised that our Bern should plead guilty to the charge and ask for his previous good conduct to be considered. There was a little light hearted banter as when asked by the clerk to take the oath our Bern added; 'So help me god.' To which the JP interjected with a wry smile; 'I do not think he will be necessary in this case.' Charlie the only witness described the Sunday afternoon action of us three boys including seeing our Bern take away a 'roll' of brattice cloth which he later identified as being used to roof a rabbit hutch at 20 Devonshire Street. He also added that he had been systematically 'terrorised' by the defendant firing a gun at him. Our Bern, as directed, pleaded guilty to stealing the brattice cloth but qualified it by saying it was a small piece that had been discarded, and then explained to the court about the 'scam' we pulled on Charlie with the pretend shooting. The JP explained to Bernard the seriousness of trespassing and also the thoughtlessness of tormenting an elderly person who honestly thought that he was being shot at, which the JP though was the more serious offence. Mum said it looked bad for Bernard at that point but the JP went on to say considering that this was a first offence and he had the support of good and caring parents he would dismiss the case with a fine of 7s.6d for the brattice cloth. It seemed odd to me that neither I nor Roger were brought to book as we were equally guilty and I particularly was conscious of our Bern 'carrying the can' for us.

That building development period of some eighteen months also marked the end of our childhood and by 1950 we were never again to run wild across the back fields or through the woods at Sheepbridge, instead we turned to more mature pursuits. In the years to come Keith Tasker would always introduce me to people we met socially, generally in a pub, as the West End kid who 'declared war' on the new residents of Kendall Road. Of course this was a symbolic gesture and was influenced by the many western films where the Native American's were always fighting a losing battle to retain there hunting land against the encroachment of the white man. I was a sort of latter day King Canute making a futile attempt, by command, to stop the tide coming in.

The disappointments of that summer of 1950 was somewhat offset by the family having a first 'real' holiday when in August Dad and Mum took us to Blackpool for a week where we stayed at a Boarding House on Dickson Road run by a Miss Lee. I remember the proprietor and other guests being very friendly and one particular incident that for some reason brought forth amusement from the adults when at breakfast a young honeymoon couple were ribbed for breaking their bed. For the life of me I could not fathom out why this was considered funny.

Bernard and I spent a great deal of time at the South Shore open air bathing pool which we soon found out, to our distaste, had salt water. The diving platform was 36 feet high, and looked it to Bern and me. We decided to ascend to take a look from the top and gingerly tiptoed to the edge of the platform were immediately the lifeguard attendant blew his whistle to clear the area beneath the diving board then signalled to Bern and me that it was safe to dive. With utter consternation we decided that we dare not descend the steps and agreed to jump to save some sort of face. It seemed to me to take forever before I hit the water and received such a blow that it took all of the wind out of me. When we eventually surfaced to my amazement it was to general applause although I still felt rather stupid for 'bottling' the actual dive.

One afternoon when approaching the swimming pool we stopped to admire a small sleek white sports car with red leather upholstery; the likes of which we had never seen. It had a name badge that said 'Palm Beach'. It turned out to belong to the film star and ex-Olympic swimming champion Johnny Weissmuller who we had seen many times starring as Tarzan. He was appearing at the South Shore pool in a 'Gala Spectacular' and much to our disappointment we could not afford to see him. Whilst at the pool Bern and I entered into the Daily Mail 'Learn to swim campaign' for which we each received a certificate and medallion. As we could both swim proficiently we obtained these items under false pretences but I am sure that the newspapers organisers knew that also.

Dad always liked a mid day drink of beer and in the Tower he could get his favourite tipple of Worthington Bitter. Mum would have a glass of OBJ which many years later I discovered stood for 'Oh Be Joyful.' During our visit to the Tower we visited the Zoo which with its cages and the sweet but musty smell of wet straw reminded me of Belle Vue. On view there was a rare big cat called a Liger it was apparently a cross between a male lion and a female tiger. I left the zoo area feeling rather sorry for the animals kept in such cramped and unnatural conditions.

The weather was sunny most of the week causing a heat wave and we were able to take advantage of the seven miles of beautiful sandy beaches, although on the Friday afternoon there was a violent thunderstorm that caused Woolworths, which was situated near the Tower, to flood. On that afternoon we visited the cinema to see Walt Disney's film *Treasure Island* and Bernard and I were each given a replica 'Pieces of Eight' coin made from card.

Dad had seen a yellow and green coloured checked lumberjack style shirt in a shop at the bottom of Dixon Road and was dithering most of the week about whether to buy it. On the Friday afternoon after visiting the cinema he made up his mind to have the shirt but when we arrived at the shop it was closed and would not be open until 10am Saturday morning. Our train to Chesterfield was scheduled to depart at 10.30am on the Saturday morning so Mum arranged that she would go to the shop whilst we made our way with the luggage to the station. Mum went 15 minutes early in the hope that the shop would be open but in fact it opened 5 minutes after 10am. Mum on collection of the shirt ran all the way to the station and with only minutes to spare joined us on the platform. Dad wore that shirt for several years then passed it on to Bernard who in turn passed it on to me. That shirt never seemed to wear out and in the end Mum made used of it as a duster. That first holiday was idyllic. Both Bernard and I have been to more exotic places but that summer week in Blackpool is always the one that we most reminisce about.

Chapter 14 – Hello Sailor Boy, Who Are You Dreaming Of Tonight?

Row, row, row your boat

Gently down the stream.

Merrily, merrily, merrily, merrily

Life is but a dream.

NURSERY RHYME

Film starlet Joan Dowling with Chesterfield Sea Cadet Corps 1951
I am smallest cadet at front with Bernard on my right.

Bernard and I became regular supporters of Chesterfield FC in late 1946. We would be at the Recreation Ground, Saltergate on every other Saturday to watch their home games in the Second Division Taking our places near the centre line at the Compton Street side of the ground, in them days the attendance was around 12,000 so to get a clear view fellow supporters would help us to get a 'leg up' to the top of the roof support cross trees of the corrugated steel shelter on that side of the ground. Over the next seven seasons we were avid supporters and regularly also attended the Reserve Team Central League games played every other Saturday. We were privileged to watch a team that achieved its highest ever placing by ending the 1947 Season in fourth position in the Second Division. Their names come flooding back; Ray Middleton, Billy Kidd, Billy Whitaker, Dudley Milligan, Sid Goodfellow, Ken Booker, George Milburn, Harold Roberts, Jackie Hudson, Tom Swinscoe, Billy Linacre, Syd Ottewell and Dick Cushlow.

After the games finished we would rush home where our tea would have already been prepared by Mum, and we would eat, whilst listening to the football results on the BBC light programme broadcast of 'Sports Report edited by Duncan Mackay' pronounced by the BBC programme introducer as 'Machigh.' After tea we would rush down to Tucker's shop to buy the 'Green-Un' the Sheffield Star Saturday evening sports newspaper printed on green coloured newsprint. I was particularly fascinated by the summary of a local match, usually the Sheffield clubs, in strip cartoon format produced by 'Heap' which influenced me to emulate his technique with little success but I do remember getting a close likeness of George Farm the then Rangers and Scotland goalkeeper. I also remember our bedroom wall displaying a double centre page pull-out of an headline that was titled 'Flying Ballet at Hillsborough' and depicted Redfern Frogatt the Wednesday forward diving horizontally to head the ball into the net. Of course my all time favourite player was Gordon Dale the consummate deliverer of a ball from the wing whose skills could not unfortunately prevent the slide of Chesterfield FC's relegation to the third division north, and his subsequent departure from Saltergate.

One evening in the summer of 1948 I met Pete Wright and Fergy Finney coming down Devonshire Street both dressed in Royal Naval uniform. It turned out that they had joined the Chesterfield Unit of the Sea Cadet Corps and had just been issued with their 'blues.' I had at that time no interest in joining any organisation, but in this case, though it worth it to be able to wear this particular uniform. Both me and our Bern went along with the two lads to the next parade and signed the registration forms to become Sea Cadets. I thought that I would receive my uniform there and then but was terribly disappointed when told we would have to wait three weeks for then to arrive. That three weeks waiting seemed interminable and I was most enviable of Pete and Fergy wearing their smart uniforms whilst I was still parading in 'civvies.'

As I have stated my sole motive in joining the Sea Cadets was to wear the uniform but to my surprise I thoroughly enjoyed every aspect of the training and social activities and was to remain a cadet for nearly four years. In 1948 the unit had temporary headquarters in Elder Yard located off Saltergate and at the time of our joining were in the process of relocating to larger premises near the bottom of Lordsmill Street, and to expedite procedures all of the ships company helped with the refurbishment of Training Ship Chesterfield, later to be re-commissioned as TS Danae. To recognise the team effort of our re-location to Lordsmill Street the unit was awarded its first ever efficiency pennant.

On entry to the Unit I was assigned to Lieutenant Commander Fry, Officer in command of Port Watch. The Commanding Officer was Lieutenant Commander Lucas and Lieutenant Sharman was Officer in command of Starboard Watch. The other two officers were Lieutenants Truswell and Allsop. There were also several junior Non Commissioned Officers whose names now escape me. We would meet Tuesday and Thursday evenings mainly for instructional periods then Sunday mornings where the whole ship's company would parade for worship followed by colour party drilling and band practice as we had to attend many ceremonial gatherings in and around Chesterfield including Remembrance Sunday and Trafalgar Day. On such occasions I marched with a side drum whose steel thigh brace would rub my left leg raw. On occasional Sundays we would assemble at Walton Dam Boathouse were the Unit kept a very heavy Whaler which when rowing strained every muscle as we strived to propel it forwards.

Reginald Fry, my watch officer was a stickler for discipline and took his duties seriously, but a fairer man you would never meet. Reg by his own example moulded me from a rag tag urchin into an able youth who took care of appearance and pride in being a member of TS Chesterfield.

In them days we wore 'bell bottom' trousers that had to have the mandatory ironed seven horizontal creases and summer dress hat, belt and gaiters 'Blanco' whitened.

After about twelve months I was promoted to the rank of Able Seaman for passing examinations in general seamanship including knots and navigation. To help with this examination Bernard and I built a model of Plymouth Harbour, and Sound, on which were placed the various marker buoys that defined the safe passage ways in and out of the Naval Establishment. After a further year I was again promoted to the rank of Leading Seaman having gained a qualifying grade in signalling using Semaphore and Morse code. Semaphore, using flags, was relatively easy to achieve by just memorising the different arm positions. Morse code, where a combination of dots and dashes were transmitted through the ether by use of a Morse key was much more difficult than semaphore in that the message was sent in a rhythmic combination to distinguish each letter. This distinctive rhythm was difficult to learn and took me personally six months to become proficient.

On a dark rainy Thursday evening in January 1950 the Devonshire Street cadet group were on the way to Lordsmill Street for a normal evening parade and had just alighted off the bus at Elder Way when we saw the Sheffield Star news bulleting board headlines that the submarine HMS Truculent was missing in the Thames Estuary. Normally we would have just thought nothing of it but being in the Sea Cadets it became rather poignant. I still remember my feeling of apprehension of that night and the uneasiness of the entire ships company during that parade. Our worse fears were founded when in the following days it was announced that the boat was declared lost with its crew of 54 together with 14 civilian admiralty workers. It was a blow that affected not only next of kin but also the entire naval personnel and associated shore establishments such as our own Unit, as ten days after the tragic incident, on the week following the previous Sunday we held a special remembrance service that was deeply moving and which I still remember with sadness. Just after this incident our Bernard went to Birkenhead to witness the launch of the aircraft carrier Ark Royal. When I eagerly asked him what sort of experience it had been he said; 'We were assembled on a platform in front of which was a huge grey wall obscuring our view of the ship. It wasn't until this wall moved away that I realised that this wall was the Ark Royal.'

Normally, of course, cadet life was one of fun and excitement with a great camaraderie, and me being the youngest getting extra special treatment, and help from my fellow cadets, but not from the officers may I point out. Many of the friends that I made during my four year period I still occasionally run into, but as many, actually on reaching the age of eighteen made the Royal Navy their career and seemed to drop out of circulation.

There was a 'special' bonus for the Devonshire Street cadet group as on the parade evenings of Tuesday and Thursday, as after the parade finished at 9pm, we would sneak into the Elder Way side entrance of the Victoria Cinema to catch the greater part of the feature film. The Elder Way entrance was to the cheap front stall seats and it was normal to see folk leaving their seats to visit the toilet located down the stair next to the pay booth. We would hide our hats under our greatcoats and make our way past the then vacated pay booth and upstairs to the stalls entrance where we would, one by one, enter and take any seat unoccupied. Later we would all join up. Sometimes the usherette would get wise and then a pursuit would follow where we would disappear under the seat and re-emerge in a different place. Eventually she would give up and let us view the film without hindrance. On one such week we actually found ourselves paying twice to see the same film as on the Tuesday evening, as normal, we sneaked in to see Debra Paget starring as the Princess Kalua in a south sea island film setting called '*Bird Of Paradise*' which had a climax were she had to sacrifice herself by jumping into an erupting volcano to appease the gods of her forbears. Debra was again co-starring with Jeff Chandler after their appearance the previous year in the excellent western '*Broken Arrow*' were she similarly played the part of an Apache maiden called Sonseeahray, as Jeff Chandler, taking the part of Cochise, tells James Stewart; 'The name means Morning Star.' As adolescents we were all 'in love' with Debra Paget and the film Bird Of Paradise was so emotional with the ending of her taking farewell of her French Lover and plunging into the inferno, that we had to see this film over and over again on the consecutive days Tuesday through Friday.

In the autumn of 1951 Mr Dixon the manager of the Regal Cinema, later named the ABC, invited the Unit to present a colour party display on stage as an introduction of the film *Horatio Hornblower RN* starring Gregory Peck as the eponymous hero. On the same evening, and before our display, the young glamorous film star Joan Dowling appeared on stage and gave a cabaret show in aid of promoting her latest film *Murder without Crime*. I had see Joan when she was thirteen year old co-starring in my very favourite 1947 film *Hue and Cry* and was excited at the prospect of watching her live performance. The evening got more exciting as the Unit was invited to be photographed with Joan and Mr Dixon after which she repaired to the upper auditorium to sign autographs. As I took my place in the queue to get my autograph I could actually hear my heart throbbing in my ears and was finding it difficult to breath, and as I finally met the vision that was Joan Dowling dressed in a sparkling white full length evening gown surmounted by a white fur stole, I became dumb struck as she took of my hat and placed it on her head whilst saying to me in a cockney accent; 'Hello sailor boy, who are you dreaming of tonight?' I stood there transfixed whilst trying desperately to give her an answer, but to no avail the words would not form. Taking the hat off her head she autographed the inside then placed it back on my head and gave me a kiss on the cheek and dismissed me with; 'Bye, bye cutie.'

Talking about glamorous girls, one Sunday morning in the summer of 1950 the Devonshire Street gang, as was becoming a regular habit, were attending a swimming session at Stand Road open air pool when Harry Fish's daughter, Rosalie, made an appearance in a white terry towelling bikini two piece swim suit, an action which was sensational for that period in time. She had just come back from a vacation on the French Riviera sporting a tan that set the white bikini off to perfection. It is difficult in this modern era where 'anything goes' to appreciate the shock then of viewing so much exposed toned flesh and the risqué provocation suggested by her choice of swim wear, as never before had we been privileged to see such a flimsy garment. Most young women were still attired in a woollen one piece nineteen thirties style swimming costume with a few able to afford the then 'modern' one piece suit has worn by the swimming film star Esther Williams. Ethel Kennel, a near neighbour of ours, was one such young lady who at that time was a fellow member of our Monday evening swimming club.

After Arthur Lucas retired as superintendent at Stand Road his position was taken by the younger and forward thinking Jack Mobbs who persuaded Bernard and me to become members of the British Railway Swimming Club which also ran courses in life saving in association with requirements of the Royal Life Saving Society. Our Bern enrolled for the Bronze Medallion award for life saving, a course that took three months to complete with minimum age requirement of 14 years at test. I not being eligible by age for the medallion course opted for the Society's Life Saving Diploma, a course that lasted six weeks with minimum age of 12 years. As there were no younger persons on my course I was paired with Ethel Kennel, then 18 years old, which of course, I was delighted about. Ethel was a strong and capable swimmer who would stand no nonsense from the likes of me, and in fact, we did go on to make an excellent pairing and completed the course successfully.

As members of the British Railway Swimming Club we also competed in local swimming galas specialising in freestyle events and diving. We also, along with Peter Wright and Roger Huckerby from our Devonshire Street gang, represented our Secondary Schools at inter-school swimming galas. Our Bern excelled at platform diving and won every event that he entered, and may I say wherever he appeared he attracted a following of young girls that did not sit well with the local youths. I unfortunately often caught the backlash of their animosity. For instance one evening I had been to the Chesterfield Technical College and was waiting for a bus outside the Regal Cinema when a group of youths spilled out of the cinema. I of course recognised them as a group of self

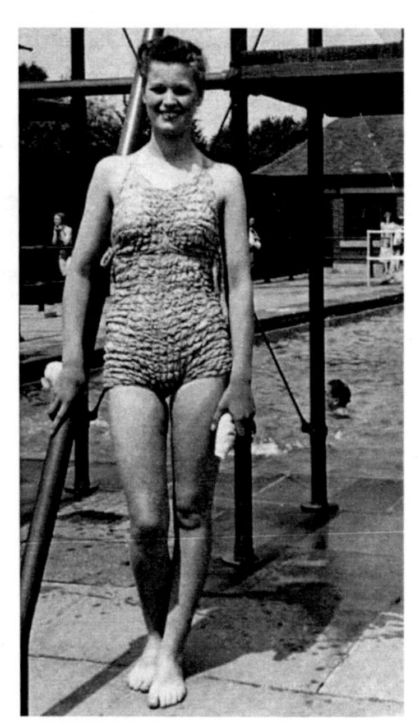

Ethel Kennel – Stand Road Pool – 1949

styled tearaways from the Brushes area of Old Whittington led by one Barry (Bagger) Lilly. Bagger, who was two to three years older than me, swaggered up to me with 'his gang' in tow and turning to them said; 'Look who we've got here. Its Bragger Ellis's little brother.' I actually though that I was in for a right pasting, but to tell the truth I had never actually seen Barry Lilly get into a fight until much later when he was inadvertently caught up in a fracas during a dance held one Friday evening at the Hollingwood Hotel, but that's another story. As it happened he contented himself with making verbal threats of what he would do to our Bern. I scornfully suggested that he should repeat these idle threats when he came face to face with my brother. He gave me a hollow laugh and sauntered away.

Barry had on a previous occasion tried to wind me up. I would be about 12 years old and was in the Lyceum Billiard Hall playing a game of snooker with Keith (Baldy) Wright, Pete's younger brother. Sat patiently waiting for the table was a young lad about the same age as me who I knew vaguely from the Brushes by name of Pete Carlisle. Up saunters Barry Lilly making his way to talk to Pete, I think they were near neighbours or even may have been relatives. On seeing me at the table he said to Pete, in my hearing; 'Aren't you afraid? There's a tough guy there from the West End.' Again, it was like a scene from a movie, in particular *The Kentuckian* where the 'baddy' Walter Matthau, a whip swinging braggart, goads a young lad to pick a fight with the son of the eponymous hero played by Burt Lancaster. As similarly happened with Rob Troth, Pete ignored the prompting to instigate a fight. In later years Barry had quite a testing period in his life and I am pleased to say that he and I are amicable and friendly with each other on the few occasions that we meet each other on Church Street, Old Whittington.

In the summer of 1951 our Bern had left Peter Webster School and commenced work as an apprentice Plater (Boiler Smith) with Sheepbridge

Engineering. I myself was laden down with school homework so Bernard and I decided with a little regret it was the right time to take leave of our tenure as Sea Cadets which we had enjoyed for some three and a half years. Very soon we would as a family make a more important decision to leave the West End. But I am getting ahead of myself for I must now return to the summer term at Gilbert Heathcote School and the prospect of the 11+ examinations.

Chapter 15 – Secondary Education And New Whittington

Be Careful to leave your sons well

Instructed rather than rich

For the hopes of the instructed are

Better than the wealth of the ignorant.

EPICTETUS

Greek Philosopher

Class 4A Peter Webster School 1952 – Dave Benton eight from left back row, Albie Newall second from right back row, Tommy Deacon fourth from right middle row, Derek Robotham second left front row. I am far right front row.

Author age 14 years.

I recall a warm May afternoon in 1949 that my particular class of pupils at Gilbert Heathcote were assembled in Mr Holmes classroom situated at the rear corner of the main school building to commence a series of tests, the outcome of which would decide out future level of education. At that time I do not remember any member of staff explaining the importance, or significance, of these tests, and it was at a much later date when the results were revealed and we were told as a group who had, and who had not passed the Eleven + examination, that I was informed that I was a failure. It would have made not the slightest difference to the end result had I been made aware of its importance for I knew that I had given of my best. Even so I felt deflated with the result considering that I myself had every confidence that I had achieved a good overall standard, as was the norm for all my previous school work.

After the results were read out our headmaster Mr Powell gave me an envelope addressed to my parents. I naturally assumed it contained written confirmation of my failure. In fact it was a letter requesting my parents to make an appointment to see Mr. Powell. In the event it was Mum and me who found ourselves sat facing the headmaster. Mr Powell explained to Mum that although I had not met the overall requirements for entry into the Chesterfield Grammar School due to my achieving an average written English test, my Arithmetic result was amongst the top 10% and he felt that on his recommendation that I would be accepted for entry to the newly built Chesterfield Junior Technical school situated in the grounds of William Rhodes School at Boythorpe. With Mum's agreement Mr Powell set up an appointment to have an interview with Mr Stevens, the headmaster of the William Rhodes and Junior Technical School sites.

The 1944 Education Act proposed the introduction of Technical Schools to to establish a tripartite system of secondary education consisting of Grammar, Secondary Technical and Secondary Modern. The Technical School was closely linked to the world of industry and commerce in providing a general education with special emphasis on technical subjects. It was definitely more in touch with reality than the Grammar Schools and certainly more specifically geared to preparing the pupils for their trade after leaving school. It is difficult to imagine why this educational experiment was not successful. At inception there was a lack of qualified teachers and this must be seen as one cause for its lack of success. When I joined the school in September of 1949 the intake consisted of only two classes 1A and 1E. The pupils of Class IA resided in the Borough. The 1E pupils coming from outside the Borough and were 'bussed' in, and left 30 minutes earlier in the afternoon than the rest of the school.

On arrival for my interview at William Rhodes School Mum and I were greeted by Mr Reid, Senior Teacher of Craft and Design, who escorted us on a tour of the Junior Technical site. The building, which was newly erected, had a silhouette that resembled an aircraft carrier being a long low single level block with a two level structure at its centre. At the rear end was a purpose equipped Drawing Office classroom adjacent to a large workshop area that housed work benches and 12 Alfred Herbert metalworking lathes. Next in line were two Mathematics classrooms then the central two story Art and Design studios. Forward of the art block were two classrooms for teaching English language followed by purpose equipped laboratories for teaching Physics and Chemistry. Existing facilities in the main William Rhodes block was utilised for teaching Humanities, Biology and Gymnasium work. Mr Reid's courteous, enthusiastic and friendly manner throughout the tour gave me a sense of desperately wanting to be apart of this inspiring educational establishment and as he took leave of us at the Headmaster's Secretary's office he said that he would look forward to me joining the school in September.

The Headmaster, Mr Stevens, on first acquaintance seemed to me to be an aloof and charm less individual, not at all like the friendly person Mr Powell had described to Mum and me. After he had lectured us on the ideals and ethos of this new system of education and the necessity of prospective pupils meeting the criteria of his own exacting standards I was by now thinking that by making me feel uncomfortable and inadequate, we would spare him the awkward duty of rejection by voluntarily leaving his office by choice. At this point the tone of the interview seemed to change as he invited me to talk about myself and by his gentle prompting I managed to inform him that I was a Sea Cadet, keen swimmer and enjoyed outdoor pursuits such as bird watching. I then told him that I was also interested in art and design and had my own personal workshop. When asked what I was currently working on Mum interjected by saying that I just built for her a model of a horse drawn mail coach from a design in the Hobbies handbook. I believe to this day that Mum's interjection and Mr Powell's recommendation secured me my place at the Junior Technical School. Mr Stevens's offer of a placement, which by my excited reaction Mum knew that I so desperately wanted, verbally accepted. Mr Stevens went on to inform Mum that she would receive a formal letter within a few days from his Secretary together with particulars of general information, school uniform and kit requirements.

Those few waiting days were tinged with alternating thoughts of excitement and doubt but finally to my great relief the letter arrived confirming my application had been successful. There was a bit of a shock when Mum read the appendage sheet listing school uniform requirement which consisted of: Blazer, cap, tie, two pair of grey trousers, two grey shirts, four pair grey socks, two white vests, and pair of navy blue shorts, gym pumps and black shoes. Addition items were satchel, pen, pencil and geometry set to including drawing instruments. All items could be obtained from John Turner the Chesterfield outfitters for around £12.00. Mum said not to worry as there was still eight weeks before I started school and she would find the money somehow. It was rather different with Dad, from the onset he was not enthusiastic about me attending a school miles from home with the expense of bus fares and school meals to find for he knew our Bernard was quite happily settled in at Peter Webster School on Whittington Moor incurring no expense at all. When Dad read the letter and requirement of finding such a huge sum of money he immediately 'put his foot down' and said I could not accept the placement. Mum argued that there would be no expense on bus fares as Mr Stevens Secretary had told her that the school would apply to the Borough Council to obtain for me a free bus pass. She also argued that I would be taking packed lunches to save having to find dinner monies. Even so Dad would not change his mind on the matter of wasting money on a school uniform when there was a perfectly adequate school down the road that did not make these ridiculous demands. Mum kept her council and in September I started at the Chesterfield Junior Technical School attired in the mandatory uniform with a leather satchel hanging from my shoulder. In the event I also always had a hot school meal, but I am not sure Dad was ever aware of this.

It never passed through my mind at that time that by choosing to attend a different school to the rest of the boys in Devonshire Street it would be the cause of alienation between myself and my life long friends as my new social life left me little time to 'range the streets with the lads.' I frequently stayed weekends at either the homes of Alan Bown or Colin Glossop, my class mates at William Rhodes. Weekday evenings were mostly took up with homework or extra curricular pursuits. I believe that my two closest friends Peter Wright and Roger Huckerby took exception to what they perceived as my rejection of the old values and became indifferent to me henceforth.

I was, and always will be a 'kid from the West End.'

My final assembly at Gilbert Heathcote Junior School was unexpectedly quite emotional as the whole school had gathered to say goodbye to the senior boys. I cannot now recall the words of Mr Powell but they were on the lines of

'Go forth from here but always uphold the standard of behaviour learned at Gilbert Heathcote and always be proud of our school.' The whole congregation then sang the closing hymn:

"Lord, dismiss us with Thy blessing
Thanks for mercies past receive;
Pardon all, their faults confessing
Time that's lost may all retrieve;
May Thy children
Ne'er again Thy Spirit grieve."

Let Thy Father-hand be shielding
All who here shall meet no more;
May their seed-time past be yielding
Year by year a richer store;
Those returning
Make more faithful than before."

I found it most difficult to sing that last verse of the hymn as my innermost feelings began to get the better of me, thoughts of never seeing my teachers again especially Mr. Powell the first person outside of my immediate family to really understand my aspirations. These thoughts filled within me an overwhelming void and yearning to not leave the comfort of the fold that was my school. I have always remembered that morning and particularly that hymn that brought about such emotional feelings in a young boy. Many years later when I was about to take up my first teaching post in Cornwall I telephoned Eric Powell to thank him for his kindness, interest and the guidance that he had given to me, a rag-a-muffin boy, at Gilbert Heathcote, and told him that I was about to embark on a career in teaching. His never to be forgotten response was 'Brian, you must be mad.'

William Rhodes School had a four house system designed to foster pride in achievement through inter-house competitive rivalry. On that first day of arrival at school the new pupils were assigned to a particular house, mine was Faraday were I made the acquaintance of two very different boys, the slightly built, but athletic, Alan Bown was the studious type from Dukes Drive, Newbold and the more boisterous and extrovert Colin Glossop from Cutthorpe Road, Four Lane Ends, We three would remain close friends for the duration of my time at William Rhodes as we were also in the same form 1A. The houses were named after three distinguished engineers and a scientist namely; Outram, Brindley, Mitchell and Faraday. Throughout the years I always represented Faraday in swimming, discus and javelin, as I did also the School at the Chesterfield Schools Athletics Meetings held annually at the Queens Park and the Inter-Schools Swimming Gala held at The Central Schools swimming pool. Eric Irvine the PE Master coached track and field athletics with Alan Bown (Javelin and Discus), Keith Newton (Shot Putt) and me competing in the field events. Eddie Holdsworth coached the school swimming team the backbone of which was Barry and Graham Tingay, Keith Newton and I. Particularly in swimming I had mixed emotions for I was, for first time in my life, competing against my friends from Devonshire Street representing Peter Webster School, the school that nearly always took the overall trophy, their main rivals being Tapton House School. These two schools always seemed to meet also in the final of the Clayton Challenge Shield, the Chesterfield Schools football knockout tournament, again with Peter Webster generally prevailing. It was at one of the swimming galas that I met Pat Herring, who was an ever present member, and captain of the Violet Markham Girls School swimming team, and was a friend of our Bernard, Peter Bond, Peter Steele and Johnny Brookes the principal team members of Peter Webster. At this meeting I recall her comments about the need for an all weather indoor pool in Chesterfield as at that time, other than the tiny Central School pool which was not open to the public, the other existing pools were all open air. Pat later went on to successfully lobby the Chesterfield Borough Council for the building of the Queens Park pool.

In class I sat along side Colin (Glogger) Glossop whose parents happened to be the next door neighbors of our Form and Mathematics teacher Ted (Thrasher) Simmons. Unfortunately Colin had not been a model neighbor, in fact he had been a right pain to Mr. Simmons for years prior to Colin's arrival at William Rhodes and this acrimony between the two was brought into the classroom. Ted Simmons had served in the Armed Forces during the Second World War and had seen action in North Africa and Italy as a Captain in the Eight Army. He was the archetype disciplinarian, being thick set, completely bald with pugnacious features, you know, those that look like a bulldog chewing a wasp. First thing in a morning to get our minds 'sharp' Thrasher would circulate the classroom randomly testing pupils with mental arithmetic questions such as ' five sixteenths as a decimal' or ' nought point three seven five as a fraction' or 'fifteen per cent of eighty.' If the correct answer was not instantly forthcoming the unfortunate individual would get a verbal rebuke of ridicule, but in the case of Colin he would be side swiped right out of his seat. Thrasher always seemed to ask Colin his question whilst standing next to me so I always had my head pressed into my shoulders as Thrasher forcefully stooped over me to get to Colin. Over the years I came to like and respect Mr. Simmons for he was an excellent teacher of Algebra, Geometry and Trigonometry who fostered in my mind the power and use of mathematics the nature of which I pursued long after I left William Rhodes.

My History Teacher, Mr. Carr was an inspirational orator as he conjured up visions of Ancient Egypt or The Land of the Two Rivers in a quiet cultured voice that always fired my imagination and imparted pure enjoyment during his lesson periods. In appearance he had a debonair look and closely resembled the actor Peter Bowles who starred as Richard DeVere in the TV comedy 'To the

the Manor Born.' The other small thing that I recall was that Mr. Carr housed his fountain pens in an old leather cigar case that was always visible in his suit breast pocket. Later to my cost I realised the wisdom of this when my own fountain pen leaked and badly stained a rather expensive sport coat that even at this time I cannot bear to discard. It was whilst I sat dreamily listening to Mr Carr, in my first year, that I was summoned one afternoon to the gymnasium to compete in the mandatory school boxing tournament organised by Eric Ervine. I was to compete in the flyweight division and box a single one three minute round refereed by Eric and watched by a group of fourth year pupils from the William Rhodes site. My opponent was Alan (Titch) Laking a William Rhodes fourth year pupil. The round seemed to take an interminable time before thankfully the bell rang signalling the end of the fight, only to be informed that the judges had scored the contest even. Eric instructed the two of us, much to my consternation, that it would be necessary to box a further three minutes. During this further physical exertion the crowd of fourth year boys, who had supported Alan in the first round gradually started to shout encouragement and applaud my efforts, maybe because I was the obvious underdog. At the end of this extra round we were both physical drained and could no muster an effective punch between us. As we stood in the centre of the ring giving support to each other there was in that moment forged a mutual respect, which I later realised was the whole point of the tournament. It did not matter to me, and I suspect also my opponent, when the judges returned a majority points win in favour of Alan for I left the ring to a rousing round of applause and cheering.

Mr. Ashley-Cooper, a stooped middle aged and sharp featured individual whose formidable look was enhanced by sallow skin, crinkly iron grey hair and wearing heavy horn rimmed spectacles was my English teacher who took great delight in marking a pupil's homework whilst the unfortunate boy had to stand adjacent to him. Any grammatical or punctuation mistakes would be signalled by a side swipe to the boys thigh inflicted by a small cricket bat followed by audible correction repeated three times over. It was always with trepidation that I presented my homework for marking. My lack of confidence in English grammar engendered by the actions of Ashley-Cooper made mandatory referral of dictionary to ascertain my correct spelling of every word that I submitted. Even the most ordinary common usage words such as the definite article 'the' were scrupulously checked, and then double checked. Such was my fear of this tyrant. Fortunately I among many others had to endure Mr. Ashley-Cooper only for the first year of school. My future English teacher was to be the amenable Norman Hoddle an enigmatic and excellent teacher who taught me to enjoy the subject and the appreciation of poetry. At Easter time 1951 I along with a group of second year pupils went on an eighteen day field trip through Shropshire, Herefordshire and Mid Wales organised by Norman together with Messrs Herring and Holdsworth. We went by train to Birmingham then changed trains for Shrewsbury. The two hour waiting time at the gloomy war damaged Birmingham New Street Station proved an absolute delight to the many train spotters in our group; unfortunately I was numbered amongst them. Commencing at Shrewsbury we hiked down to Ludlow then on to Llandrindod Wells staying overnight in various Youth Hostels. Most of the countryside we walked through was rural and remote and the profusion of wild life was semi-tame. I remember walking right up to several ground nests without disturbing the sitting birds. It was also the first time that I had seen wild deer close up and again they seemed oblivious to our presence. One hot afternoon we were approaching farmland and as a courtesy the staff sought permission from the owner to cross his land. The owner was a 'gentleman farmer' and made us most welcome by offering us refreshment of iced orange juice and allowed us to cool off by wallowing in the nearby shallow River Arrow. He did warn us to be careful as the river was very cold at this time of year. Our boisterous group ignoring the caution plunged into the river and suffered immediately from the shock of the extremely cold water which imparted a numbing pain to our legs. Nevertheless it was a glorious unforgettable afternoon and I often think of the generous natured gentleman who was a perfect host to a complete group of strangers. There were a couple of rather humours happenings whilst on this field trip which I will describe; The first occurred when arriving at the Ludlow youth hostel we were given an hour free time before supper to explore the castle which is situated on a raised hillock. Colin Glossop and I found that a pair of ravens had nested on the local cliff outcrop and to get a better view I started to climb down the rock face which in the damp evening air was very slippery. Of course I lost my footing and slid over the edge of the rock ridge landing in a patch of brambles below. I sustained only minor grazing but on arrival back at the hostel Norman insisted that he take me to the local cottage hospital to get a check up. On arrival we were greeted by an elderly nurse whose garb surely belonged to a former age. After a cursory examination she told Norman that I would have to an injection against tetanus. She re-appeared with an enormous needle and there was no standing on ceremony as she plunged this enormous instrument into my bottom and proceeded to pump my bottom full of liquid the sight of which caused Norman to faint. Many years later I met Norman again when I did my first teaching practice at William Rhodes. On greeting me the first thing he said was; 'Do you remember that old battleaxe with the bloody great needle?' The other occasion was when we were using local ordinance survey maps to plot our daily journeys and at one instance a lane indicated on the map that we needed to take as the shortest route to our next youth hostel was completely overgrown with nettles. To save making a long detour by road it was decided by the staff that we would risk trespassing by following the course of the lane by walking through the adjacent fields whose stone wall bordering the lane to save time as it was late afternoon. We had gotten about quarter of a mile along the fields when there was an audible rumble that grew louder by the second. To our consternation we were being targeted by a herd of young bullocks who were charging down the field toward us. Norman shouted for everyone to take cover in the lane. Everyone including staff were attired in short sleeved shirts and shorts and had to 'wade' about two hundred yards through the dense growth of nettles before emerging into an adjoining road. Everyone had severe nettle rashes on arms and legs and was completely exhausted from our exertions. Norman located a telephone box and arranged for a local coach driver to pick us up. On arrival at the youth hostel the only medication they had was one bottle of camomile lotion which had to be liberally diluted in cold water to spread around the group. That night we lay in our bunks with burning hot limbs but we could all see the funny side of our afternoon jaunt.

Modern languages were the domain of Gerard Denly a lanky young man with a swarthy complexion topped with jet black crinkly hair, who had just returned from a spell teaching in Spain. This was a time before mass package holidays, or indeed any travel abroad, so it was far sighted of the Headmaster to appoint Gerard to teach Spanish and German, as the norm was French and German. I still vividly remember Gerard's introductory lesson as he wrote on the blackboard 'Pedro y Rosa son hermano y hermana' which he then pronounced and then orally translated into English. This bold experiment was like the Technical School initiative destined to be withdrawn after a few short years.

I always looked forward to the afternoons spent in the Art Studio under the tutelage of Mr Scouthern who was an accomplished fine arts painter and sculptor. Mr Scouthern encouraged us to experiment with and explore different media effects and to my great delight I found that I had a liking for clay modelling. I shared a bench with Barry Marsden who had a flair for sketching. I remember one afternoon asking him to illustrate a scene for me from the book 'Last of the Mohicans' which had always been a favourite of mine. With a few deft strokes from his pencil Barry produced a series of pictures depicting the fight between Magua and Major Duncan Haywood. Haywood with rakish tricorn hat and Magua with scalp lock flying gave the scenes realist impressions of ongoing action between the two protagonists. Barry went on to become an authoritative social historian and local archaeologist with many publications to his credit.

It was also a sheer delight to be taught Engineering Drawing and Design by Mr Reid and his assistant teacher, Mr. Rowbotham, who instructed the class in Machine Shop practice although I did get very bored once when it took me nearly two weeks to achieve a passable flat surface on a piece of mild steel using a file. The flatness was tested by rubbing the steel on a 'blue' block, which imparted a coloured dye to the high points. I silently cursed each time I filed off the dye marked area only to see, when rechecked, the dye appear in another area. I am sure that I never really did get that accursed block of metal flat. Mr.Reid related his teaching to aspects of real situations that needed investigation and then design solutions. This approach was certainly stimulating and an added perk was that often we would find ourselves 'out of school' on some research project. Such a project evolved out of a hypothetical discussion about perpetual motion in June 1951. As an introduction to the graphical plotting of a cycloid Mr Reid displayed a plywood model of two differing tracks joined side by side and having identical start and end points. One track was a curve the other was a shorter straight line track. Just imagine the two tracks as a strung archery bow leaned against a wall. At the top of each track were identical ball bearings in a starting gate and at their bottom were two retractable finishing flag posts. The question posed was; 'When released which ball bearing will reach its finishing post first?' Yes, of course we all know the answer is the one on the straight line track because it has a shorter distance to travel. When simultaneously released I was gob smacked to see the ball on the curved track, although starting slower soon accelerated past its neighbour to win by a 'distance.' This track was a special curve called a cycloid which has numerous applications in engineering design the most common of which is the curvature of gear teeth sides. This curve can be mathematically generated by applied complex equations and knowledge of calculus way beyond our limitations at that time but can simply be plotted graphically. If you imagine a hoop that has a mark painted on its rim, then when the hoop is rolled the path of the mark traces out a cycloid. Enough of this prattle which was deemed necessary to illustrate the unorthodox but effective team teaching methods employed by staff at the Junior Technical School in the late forties and early fifties. The ball bearing race was to illustrate the accelerative characteristics of a cycloid and maybe to use this as a basis for researching and designing a perpetual motion machine. (A machine that produces more energy than it consumes, therefore in theory it can run forever.) We had already covered the efficiency of machines, in our physics lessons and were aware that such a machine was not possible but the challenge was irresistible and we were determined to prove the eminent scientist wrong. In fact the project was evolved to introduce us to work as a team in research and shared design idea's which was deemed mandatory. The inevitable failure to actually produce a perpetual motion machine was incidental. The team teaching had a highly integrated forward planning system and this project was planned to coincide with the Biology Department's visit to the Northern Aquarist Show held annually at Belle Vue, Manchester. The school ran several extra curricular clubs including the three I was a member of; Chess, Philately (stamp collecting) and Tropical Fish Keeping. As a member of the latter I was included on the visit accompanied by three members of staff; Mr Hoddle, Mr Herring and Mr Reid. After visiting the show Mr Reid took me and a group of pupils from my class to the funfair section of Belle Vue to look in detail at the roller coaster rides especially the BOBS. Mr Reid explained that the cars were hauled to the uppermost point of the structure by a winch and then released to travel around the structure under their own momentum. We observed that the cars just managed to reach the top of each successive curve crest before gathering speed on the downward side gaining momentum to just surmount the next and then the ever diminishing series of curves. The acceleration and imparted momentum necessary to complete this long ride was gained by making the curves of cycloid form. As I stood there and pondered this wonder of engineering my thoughts were of the genius who had actually discovered the properties of the cycloid, how on earth was it achieved or did it evolve by a series of steps. I had of course seen this structure on a previous occasion but was completely ignorant to the intricacies involved in making it work and took it just for granted as I did the miracle of the spoken and written word. Our problem was to fathom a way of returning a ball bearing under its own momentum to its start point after completion of its journey round a track to create a periodic cycle that was perpetual in its motion. We tried to utilise the weight of the ball bearing to pivot the whole structure, then a system of levers and springs and a whole series of other weird and wonderful ideas. No we did not crack the laws of gravity or overcome frictional drag but we had a lot of fun trying and learned a tremendous amount about human ingenuity.

Biology taught by Mr Herring in a classroom that was part of the old school complex and overlooked the school playing fields. I was fortunate in that I sat at the back of the classroom near the window for here were located two tropical aquariums and in the wall a bee hive that had a glass viewing panel. In them days, unlike today with thousands of species to choose from, there was just a few live bearing fish available such as platys and guppies and I would sit entranced watching the antics of the aquariums inhabitants especially the tiny baby platys darting in and out of the dense foliage. Mr Herring also kept common Indian green stick insects that he sold for three pence each. Much to Mums disgust I always kept a couple in a glass sweet jar that I begged of Bob Hayes our grocer. The insects were about six inches long and were very hard to see amongst the privet braches that they fed on for they looked like dead twigs until they moved. It always caused a laugh when showing the insects to newcomers for they generally thought I was pulling their leg as it appeared that the jar only contained a few privet twigs until they moved which always caused a reaction of the viewer. In my second year, and much to my own surprise, I volunteered to give a talk on Puffin's to my peer group. I cannot to this day understand why I, without coercion, readily volunteered to place myself in such a stressful situation as the days leading up to the scheduled talk I suffered constant anxiety and disturbed sleepless nights. In the event the talk seemed to be concluded in a flash and I received a 'sympathetic' applause. For two years I derived great pleasure and further understanding of a subject that I dearly loved but in the Autumn Term of my third year the subject took on a rather gruesome aspect as we commenced to study anatomy which involved dissection of frogs and rodents. I squeamishly pinned the arms and legs of a preserved frog to a dissecting board then with a scalpel made a vertical incision down its stomach and opened up the cavity by pinning the stomach skin to the board. The object of the exercise was to remove the heart which I did but this action made me feel sick. When presented with a rat that had been preserved in formaldehyde that stank to high heaven I tried to carry out the dissection but started to retch and had to leave the classroom. For the rest of my time at William Rhodes I dreaded biology lessons.

I was taught Chemistry by Mr Fawcett who I thought remote and withdrawn although most knowledgeable in subject matter. During the course of my third year Mr Fawcett committed suicide. This tragic action came as a great shock to the school community particularly to the staff for they regarded Mr Fawcett with great esteem and affection. Physics was the domain of 'Pop' Pearson a large man in every sense. His thatch of blond hair and twinkling blue eyes belied his true age and his enthusiasm for his subject was infectious. I really enjoyed Physics and thought that I had made a favourable impression on Pop with my achievement in general and particularly at the end of my second year when I came out top of the class in the yearly examination. I was therefore stunned and most surprised when he sauntered up to me and in front of the whole class he addressed me with a sneering tone; 'Ellis who have you copied off?' placing the emphasis on 'you'. This thoughtless comment influenced my outlook and attitude to both Pop Pearson and the subject and sowed the seed that made me consider my future at William Rhodes School. The paradox was that my examination marks were way ahead of any other pupils making it impossible not to have cheated. On returning to school to commence my third year Pop began systematic mind games with me that was tantamount to out and out bullying which made my school life intolerable. I had no recourse to complain of this treatment as Pop was held in great regard by the Headmaster. By half term I could stand his treatment no longer and made an excuse to Mum that the long bicycle journey to and from school was getting too much for me and I would prefer to go to Peter Webster which was a ten minute walk away. (After the 1951 general election that brought the Conservative government back to power the Chesterfield Borough Council put a levy on our bus passes and to save having to find this extra expenditure I began to cycle to school). This excuse had some credence as during the previous summer term I was caught in a violent thunder storm as I cycled home one afternoon. Being summer I had on only my shirt and trousers, the rest of the school uniform was attached to my cycle bag, and by the time I reached home I was saturated. On arrival home the door was locked so I guessed Mum would be keeping Nin company as she had a dread of thunderstorms. I found Mum and Nin in her coal house sat huddled over a candle. When Mum saw the state I was in she insisted that we should go home immediately so I could get dried off and change my clothes. Nin started screaming at Mum calling her heartless and cruel for leaving her on her own. Nin's tactic of emotional blackmail, on this occasion did not achieve its objective but Mum was ostracised for the next six months for this disloyalty. Mum, like her Mother would also use similar emotional pleas with threats of suicide if left alone on Friday nights when Dad had gone to Wheeldon Mill dog track. I of course knew these were empty threats but nevertheless I felt duty bound from a very young age and into my teens to keep her company.

Mum approached the Borough Education Department on Newbold Road with a request for a transfer from William Rhodes to Peter Webster on the grounds of hardship, which was flatly turned down. Their objection was that I was getting better education opportunity at William Rhodes which was offering me a chance to sit GCE O-Level examination at sixteen years old. Ironically two pupils from Peter Webster School, David Mott and Alan Cole, had this term been transferred to William Rhodes and placed in my form 3A. This was the first time that suitable pupils on reaching the age of 13+ were given this opportunity to escape from the Secondary School education system. Mum persistently badgered the Education Department who finally relented at the end of the Spring Term of 1952 and agreed that I would attend Peter Webster commencing the Summer Term of 1952. By this time we as a family had left the West End to move into a larger house at New Whittington. I believe Dad was quite amenable to my being transferred to Peter Webster for it meant that I would leave school at the age of fifteen at Easter 1953.

By July of 1951 our Bernard had left Peter Webster School and started work as an Apprentice Plater (Boiler Smith) in the Fabrication Shop of Sheepbridge Engineering under the tutelage of Bob Francis. Bob and his younger brother Alan, also a Plater in the same Fabrication Shop, were keen swimmers and especially proficient in synchronised high board diving, and often joined our Bern and me at the Stand Road pool. Plating fabrication was a very dirty occupation and necessitated our Bern having to bathe most evenings and change his soiled Boilersuit twice a week. We were still living in a two bedroom house with no bathroom and rudimentary laundry facilities which put pressure on our grown up family as all of us by now felt a need for privacy whilst carrying out our ablutions. The privacy strain was greatest on Mum as the only female in the household, who was also still doing the weekly washing by hand. Somehow Mum persuaded Dad that it was the right time to purchase a larger house with modern facilities. She promptly arranged to view a 1930's three bedroom with bathroom semi-detached house at the top of Dunston Lane that she had set her heart on, and was to be greatly disappointed that Dad baulked at the asking price of £1500. Dad, who delivered meat to a Butcher's shop at the top of South Street, New Whittington must have been discussing his housing problem with Mr Bellamy the butcher for when he returned home he told Mum that there was a house for sale at New Whittington which had been recommended to him. He duly purchased 135 Wellington Street, an Edwardian Semi for the sum of £800 in November 1951.

I joined class 3A at Peter Webster School in late April 1952. My class and English teacher was Owen Mason. The Headmaster was Mr Middleton and other teachers that I remember were; Messrs Hunt, Lewis, Dunkerly, Elvridge, Welfare, Hooper, Williams, Marsden, Marklew, Ball and Wells. The standard of education at Peter Webster fell well short of that I had received at William Rhodes especially in the academic subjects of English, Mathematics and Science. The structure of English language was not taught. The lessons mainly consisted of updating a journal diary and I do remember one entry as; 'Yesterday the river Po overflowed.' The current mathematics was fractions, decimals and simple logarithms, topics that I had covered in my first term at William Rhodes. General science was substituted for my previous Physics, Chemistry and Biology. Mr Williams my Mathematics teacher was sympathetic to my predicament and took time out to prepare more demanding subject matter. He also suggested that if agreeable by me he would have a word with Tom Dunkerly to persuade him to let me join his evening classes in GCE 'O' Level Mathematics. I was not really keen to give up two evenings a week of my leisure time, but our Bern had, unbeknown to me, an agenda for my future career, I was going to be an Engineering Draughtsman and to that end he insisted that I take up the offer of evening classes in an unofficial capacity that excluded my taking any external examination.

I have very few other memories of my time at Peter Webster other than being a member of the Swimming Team captained by Peter Wright that won the Challenge Cup in July 1952. Other members were Roger Huckerby and Alan Goodwin. On the whole the staff was friendly, enthusiastic and dedicated within the scope of their remit to provide a basic education, not needing the motivation and drive to prepare pupils for external examinations. There was just one sour note that exemplified a certain teacher's antipathy towards pupil aspiration. 'Art' classes were taken by Mr Wells whom I believe was a general subject teacher. Generally we were just given a piece of wall lining paper and a few wax crayons and left to our own devices. Toward the end of our final year Mr Wells had taken our class on several day visits to local factories as part of our work study. The three visits I recall were; Express Dairy where we watched two ladies stood by a conveyor belt hand filling crates with milk bottles. The stifling hot BTH Glassworks was next where we stood by a furnace and watched drenching wet young men glass blowing, then Pearson's Pottery that produced quality stone wares mainly from moulds. Pearson's did have a Design Studio were a small team of talented designers created limited edition items which impressed me greatly. After our visit to Pearson's the school received a gift from them of a large quantity of fine modelling clay intended to be used in art classes. We each received a large 'dollop' of clay which most of the class used to throw at each other as soon as Mr Wells did is usual disappearing act. When it got down to actual modelling it was limited to rolling the clay out to make a snake. I do remember that George Wright and Dave Hodgson, yes the Billy Bunter type from Gilbert Heathcote, collaborated on a snake in a tree stump. Taking the opportunity to use this media I modelled a bust of the Sioux Chief Sitting Bull. And although I say it myself it was quite pleasing to the eye. At the end of the lesson Mr Wells put in an appearance and walked round the classroom inspecting the work. When he came to me he studied the bust for a few seconds then without uttering a single word he flattened it with his right hand then walked away.

Les Welfare who taught me Music and General Science had as part of his apparatus a small electric furnace in his classroom, so me and Dave Benton, a class mate, approached Les and asked him if we could spend a few dinner times in his room to do a model project and get it fired. Dave and I had recently been to the Oxford Cinema in New Whittington to see the Robert Taylor film '*Ivanhoe*' and we both produced a wall plaque of the combat between Ivanhoe and Sir Brian De Bois-Guilbert which Les successfully fired. The plaque was mounted on one of our dining room walls for several years until my Uncle Ken, after having a hearty meal stood up, spread his arms out wide then turning knocked it off the wall and at the same time skittled a fine Derbyshire Stone Vase off the Sideboard which had been specially made by Pearson's as a present to Mum from her Uncle Ernest Lister who was then a Manager with Pearson's. Ken later also managed to shatter one of my aquariums by repeating his 'hearty meal gesture' but that is another story.

My particular class mates at Peter Webster were Derek Robotham from Shaw Street, Albert (Albie) Newell, Tommy Deacon, both from the Brushes on Sheepbridge, and David (Batman) Benton from New Whittington. Dave used to race around the village on a beaten up bike with a dyed black coloured flour bag that had eye slits which was pulled over his head and an old raincoat fastened round his shoulders. Dave was a very talented trumpet player and I have fond memories of listening to his Combo playing at a New Years Eve Dance at The Swanwick Memorial Hall, Old Whittington in 1952 and in particular Dave performing a solo of 'When The Saints Go Marching In' which was greeted with rapturous applause. Then walking back to New Whittington in the mild early hours of New Years Day with my then girl friend Irene Ratcliffe and accompanied by John Brothers, a friend of mine from New Whittington, and his friend Pam Murfin. This was truly blissful interlude of time as the youthful blossoming and passion of first love sped the blood coursing through my veins.

New Whittington in the early 1950s boasted a thriving scene of eleven pubs and two clubs within its small boundary. Dad and Mum opted to make the Wellington Hotel with its genial landlord Joe Gilbert as their local which they visited most evenings. The warren of streets and back alleys were ideal for our street games and a spot of courting the girls. I had just turned fourteen when I met my first 'serious' girlfriend. Irene Ratcliffe, who attended Mary Swanwick School and would catch the same bus as me after school as we both lived on Wellington Street. Irene at thirteen was a school year behind me but always seemed to be rather more maturely advanced than me. I 'accidentally' ran into her on my roller skates one Saturday afternoon and escorted her to the local Oxford Cinema that evening where the usherette, Mrs Tart, showed us to a double 'lovers' seat. The film as I remember was *'Bitter Rice'* an Italian film with English subtitles starring Anna Magnani. I never did get the plot. The Oxford Picture Palace was the focal point of entertainment in New Whittington, and well attended right up to its closure in the mid fifties. There was also a Dance Night for young people held Friday evenings in the old St Barnabas Church Hall at the top of Station Lane. The lady who ran the dance always wore silk or maybe satin evening dresses, and when partnering her there was a static electric interchange between us.

1952 witnessed the embryonic emergence as what we now call 'Teenagers'. I remember our Bernard being measured for a bottle green Gabardine suit from Alexander Men's Outfitters on the Chesterfield High Street, and purchasing a pair of crepe soled Brothel Creepers from Philips Shoe Shop also on the High Street. This was prior to the 'Teddy Boy' era, and was, I think, influenced by the American Pop stars Frankie Laine and Johnnie Ray. It is hard to believe in this modern era that such innocuous clothing could stir up such resentment. Bill Hewitt who owned a farm at the top of Glasshouse Lane and was one of my Dad's greyhound racing cronies on seeing is son Colin, together with our Bern and Gordon Clewly, ensconced on our settee all showing yellow or pink socks said; 'They look like bleedin' American Tomcats.' Irene always fashionable herself kept on to me to get 'grown up clothes' as I was still wearing tank top Fair Isle jumpers and grey trousers. On the 'Old Market' in New Square one Saturday morning I saw a red burgundy Corduroy jacket that was unfortunately too big for me. The stall holder directed me to a tailors workroom that was above were John Dents is now situated. The cost of the made to measure coat was to be £4 and I somehow managed to talk Mum into letting me have the money. The first evening that I wore the coat, with black slacks, to accompany Irene to the Oxford it caused quite a commotion among the elderly patrons who had the cheek to call round to see Mum on the grounds of morality. Of course this only served to strengthen my resolve to wear what I wanted. Wearing my 'coat' one Saturday evening I took Irene to a dance at the Bradbury Hall, Brampton. This was a time when Be-Bop was the latest craze and I remember watching Doreen Holmes, a young girl from Racecourse Road, dressed in a Gabardine costume demonstrating with her partner this dance to the tune '*Blacksmith Blues*' by Ted Heath's Orchestra. I kept that coat for two years before passing it on to my cousin Michael Hardy who then wore it for a further three years.

Sheepbidge Apprentices works outing to Blackpool 1952 – Back row (left to right): Tom Deacon, Walt Bennett , Ray Brownlow. Front row: Bernard Ellis, Terry Woods, Cliff Elliot.

At the beginning of 1953 I joined the Youth Club held at The Swanwick Memorial Hall, Old Whittington. Irene was not interested in coming so I went with a pal of mine Derek Hitchman. On my first visit I came face to face with a rather shy girl with whom I was instantly smitten, her name was Barbara Woodward, and co-incidentally she was in the same class as Irene at Mary Swanwick School. I instinctively knew that somehow fate would get us together and she was the girl that I would eventually marry. I met Barbara again some five years later and the rest is our history.

I left Peter Webster School at Easter time 1953 without any formal qualifications but with an excellent school report were I was placed top of class in all subjects except Music and Religious Instruction. Unlike Gilbert Heathcote there was no special leaving assembly, we just collected an official letter of discharge and left. Our Bern immediately arranged for me and he to visit the Drawing Office of The Derbyshire Carriage and Wagon Company and its subsidiary Whittington Engineering whose joint site was situated at the bottom of South Street were we met up with the Chief Draftsman Cyril Cox and his staff. After Bernard had asked Cyril all the pertinent questions and received encouraging replies our Bern intimated that he may consider letting me apply for a position in the Company. This was in the halcyon days when jobs were plentiful and you could virtually pick and choose which company suited you. Cyril then introduced us to John Plackett the Personnel Officer who discussed with Bernard the programme of training and further education opportunities on offer at the joint companies. In my particular case I was offered a position as Staff Apprentice Draughtsman. I would spend one year on the Shop Floor to familiarising myself with the products and manufacturing capabilities of both companies before transferring to the drawing office. I would be allowed one day a week (And three evenings of my own time) to attend Chesterfield Technical College were I was expected to obtain a Higher National Certificate in Mechanical Engineering. As I recall with our Bern's approval we sat down in John Plackett's office and filled in the necessary paper work. I was to report to Morris Blissett in the Jig and Tool Room at 7.30am the following Monday morning.

Chapter 16 – Whittington Engineering

Fools rush in where angels fear to tread

ENGLISH IDIOM

Peter Webster School championship swimming team October 1951. Front centre: Peter Steel with trophies. To his left Bernard, Roger Huckerby and Harold Fearn

Peter Webster School championship swimming team October 1952. Front centre: Peter Wright with trophy. To his left Roger Huckerby. Author second left front row.

The first few weeks at work were to be one of the arduous periods of my life as I tried to adjust from school hours to the long working days of 7.30am to 5.30pm Monday to Friday and 7.30am to 12.30pm Saturdays. To compound this situation Morris Blissett gave me the mind numbing task of finish shaping the profile of a press tool from an oblong of welded steel blocks that had been roughly formed on a shaping machine. I was equipped with a Desoutter air grinder and a cardboard template and sat there hour after hour making little if any progress, the only reward for my labour was a mouth full of hot burnt cinder particles. This task was in fact a demonstration to teach me a salutary lesson in patience and also to knock any youthful 'cockiness' out of me. That initial few weeks I thanked god for the presence of Cis Sharman an elderly gentleman who managed the bolt store, as he provided for me a sack bagging bed hidden behind one of his racks where I could get my head down for half hour every afternoon. I had just began to get used to, and accepting, the reality of having to work extremely long hours and forfeiting the carefree freedom of childhood, when within six weeks of starting work the coronation of our present Queen took place. New Whittington, in celebration held one gigantic children's street party which my girl friend, Irene attended but to which I was not now eligible. Still really being a kid at heart I was hugely disappointed at missing out on the celebrations, and unhappy with my lot, which unsettled me once again and took a few weeks to shake off.

At work there were of course initiation ceremonies as happens in all aspects of industry. As a child in the West End I had heard many salacious tales about the gangs of female buffers and fettlers employed in the Sheffield Steel and Cutlery trade, and sure enough I became a 'victim' that caused me real embarrassment. Morris and Ray Fiddler, a first class welder and burner, accompanied me on my first visit to the canteen with the pretext of assist me in collecting a number of mashing cans that had been filled with hot tea. The canteen cook was Mrs Booker from Barrow Hill and her assistant was Nellie Allport a petite dark haired middle aged lady from London Street, New Whittington. On entry to the canteen Ray pinned me against the wall and Morris proceeded to drop my bib and brace overalls and trousers just leaving me in underpants. At this point Nellie took up a stance in front of me and removed her overall revealing a black lace under slip. She then began to slowly raise this garment revealing matching knickers. I was too embarrassed to look so she came close and started to rub her body against mine. She then gave me a peck on the cheek and was gone. After an initial shyness toward Nellie we became the best of friends happily chatting away each time I collected the cans. I also fell for a trick by Gil Hibbert the Foreman of the Machine Shop who always addressed me, and everyone, as 'Shag'. One morning he came up to me with an empty fire bucket in his hand. Handing me the bucket he said; 'Shag, just nip down to the fitting shop and get me a bucket of blast.' In my naivety I did not question this request and preceded down the yard to the fitting shop were I met Charlie (Penguin) Birch who must have been a fixture there for donkey's years. 'Charlie Gil's sent me down for a bucket of blast.' Charlie led me to a pipe and turned a valve that released a stream of compressed air. 'Help yourself' he nonchalantly said.

I was also the butt of jokes played out by a member of the Pit Tub assembly line crew. Jimmy Greaves, no not the footballer, was the team leader and all round good guy but his number two Les Wheatcroft was a bit of a pain. Pit tub assembly was carried out adjacent to the Jig and Tool room, separated only by a wooden screen with long wooden benches on either side. One morning during my first week at work I was delivering a fixture to Jimmy when a character, which I later knew as Les Wheatcroft, was sprawled across the benches. He called me across to him and said; 'What's your name lad?' 'Brian' I replied. 'Give us you hand Brian' Les said as he smilingly offered his own hand. When I grasped it I received a juddering electric shock that reverberated through my entire body, buckling my knees, and rooted me to the spot. He had kept his other hand out of view behind his back which was holding a live electric welding iron. He also was responsible for another nasty caper. The wooden screening that separated the two work areas had small gaps between the planking and here Les would place a steel washer and 'ping' it at some unsuspecting person walking up the Jig and Tool room. The flying washers had stuck me on several occasions and one in particular caught my left ear causing an extremely painful inflammation. I was so fed up with being constantly hit I decided to retaliate. Early one morning I sat on the bench that was at our side of the screen with primed oil can and as soon as I saw the washer appear in the gap followed by Les's peeping eyes I squirted the oil full in his face. Yes, I know it was an irresponsible and dangerous act as the oil did go into his eyes which had to be treated at the ambulance room. Luckily for me, although Les suspected that I was the culprit he could not prove it.

There was a ritual at tea break every morning in the Jig and Tool room were several production operatives congregating round the pot bellied stove, irrespective of the season of the year. During the first few weeks I soon became expectant when the hooter sounded the end of break, as all the tea dregs would be thrown at me. One morning I purposely left my own drink untouched and as the dregs came over I singled out Alan (Pym) Bailey, a radial drill operator, and confronted him with my full cup. He sprinted down the room with me in pursuit. Alan made a beeline for the open end door of the Pit Tub bay but inadvertently knocked over a steel corrugated welding screen that had been placed next to the door opening, revealing the seated, slightly built figure of Albert (Ferret) Haughton, the Time and Motion Inspector. Now Jimmy Greaves had witnessed this occurrence and at once realised that Ferret had set up this screen to cover his covert action of timing pit tub assembly. For once Jimmy lost his cool and striding over to Ferret he lifted him to his feet then 'frogmarched' him to the open door and pitched him onto an area of ground that was soaked with grey lead paint that was used for 'painting' the finished tubs.

The company employed a young man who had learning difficulties as a general labourer and one of his duties was to hand paint pit tubs which was carried our in an outside sandy area. The young man was called 'Buck,' I never knew his real name. In appearance and manner he was very much like 'Trigger' the character in 'Only Fools and Horses.' I had witnessed Buck on several occasions engaged in painting the tubs and his method was to pour the paint straight out of the canister on to an exposed side of a tub then using a piece of paint and dirt sodden rag spread it with a scrubbing action. He would then apply this method to all sides and at each turn of the tub the still wet painted sides making contact with the ground would pick up a coating of sand and dirt which was absorbed into the paint. This procedure made a mockery out of the costing of painting a tub at one penny a square foot as Buck must have wasted a gallon of paint on each tub. As with every gathered group of young men there existed on the Whittington Engineering shop floor a culture of 'bragging' rights. Both Pym Bailey and Nobby Clark who were of single status and earning a substantial wage as piece work production operatives were leaders in boasting about there social life of 'wine, women and song' In their case though it was not wine but bitter beer. They had recently been to Blackpool and were enthralling us with their exploits when Buck, who generally never said a word, made the statement; 'I can drink ten pints in ten minutes.' This casual comment seemed to touch a raw nerve of Pym's inflated macho ego for he quickly retorted; 'That's f......g impossible.' 'Do yer wanna bet?' replied Buck, again in a very casual manner. It was therefore arranged that we should all congregate on the Saturday dinner time at the local pub, the Forge, as there was a combine wager of £12 bet against Buck achieving this feat. Ten pints were lined up and comfortably within the time specified Buck sank the lot with ease and with no apparent after effects. It was thought that he was able to swallow with little or no restriction due to him having a smaller than normal sized Adam's apple, or dysfunctional epiglottis, although this was just speculation.

My training in the Jig and Tool room was extensive and varied and allowed for me to interact with all other departments that used our jigs and fixtures. Typically, Jimmy Greaves raised a problem with Morris Blissett that when assembling rivet jointed pit tub bodies that the adjacent holes in two abutted plates never lined up, in fact generally you could barely see daylight between them so Jimmy had to use a drift tool to achieve alignment which cost him precious time and hence money. The rows of punched rivet holes in the plates were produced by the punching machine operator Harold Garner, who only had sight in one eye. His method was to use a lath of wood as a marking guide which had a series of drilled holes along its length set to the correct pitch sizes. This lath was placed on the plate edge and using a piece of brass tube that had been dipped in white paint he poked this through the holes to transfer the pattern onto the plate. Like most employees Harold was on piece work so he offered the 3ft x 4ft plates, which he man handled, up to the punch which was switched to a permanent on mode. The finished plates that had been punched in the semi-darkness of the machine shop invariably had witness of white paint and in some cases the complete white marking was visible. Jig and Tool design was not in the remit of the main Drawing Office but was the responsibility of Production Engineer Bob Holden and is young assistant Trevor Hadfield. Trevor would become a life long friend as was his future wife Pam, a comptometer clerk with the company. Bob designed a fixture that had a series of adjustable stops that would guarantee perfect placement of the holes and guarantee alignment when assembled. The fixture was manufactured and fitted to the punching machine and Harold was instructed on its operation which necessitated some fiddling with the stops and switching the machine on and off. Within a few days the fixture was laid idle beside the punch and Harold had reverted back to his paint marker method. The hapless Gil Hibbert seemed powerless to insist on the re-instatement of the fixture in face of Harold's voracious protest at losing money.

The press brake was operated in the same cavalier way with the safety guard removed to speed up production. The operator was an eighteen year old lad from Eckington by name of Keith Bennett.

The company had won an order to manufacture lifting jacks for the French railways. The actual fabricated lifting head of the jack had a mild steel undulating curved cover that needed a special press tool to produce it. The tool was initially manufactured to near the exact curvature of the finished cover but due to the elastic property of the thin strip of mild steel that formed the cover the tool would need to be tweaked to slightly over bend the strip that would on release from the tool spring back to the shape required. Keith was asked to press a few test pieces that I would check against a dowel pegged fixture that would only allow the desired shape to fit. We had done a few tests and were getting very near to the required shape and I asked Keith to press me three more test pieces. Throughout the run Keith had kept the press brake pedal down and had a rhythm going of press, remove, press, remove, when he suddenly turned to me saying; 'Look at this,' and presented his hands which were missing both thumbs. I actually walked him up to the ambulance room before he passed out. Returning in a shocked and dazed state of mind to the scene of the 'accident' I stood there gazing in sort of dreamlike trance at the mangled flesh and bone. I remember the only thought that passed through my head was how surprised I was that finger nails were so long. Six months would pass before I saw Keith again when he paid us a visit at work. I never saw him again.

The Blacksmiths shop was the domain of Horace (Hossy) Aaron and his striker Cocky, never knew his surname. Their main function was to drop forge components for railway wagon underfames, and strappings for wagon bodies. The environment was hot and dirty and whilst working a spell with then in a particular hot July I was sweating so much that I had trouble seeing as the perspiration poured down my face. Hossy offered me a swig out of his bottle of liquid that I supposed from its colour was Tizer. Gratefully accepting I swallowed a good mouthful before my throat constricted and I threw it all back, for it was cold stale tea that smelt and tasted revolting. Hossy and Cocky had also a lad, Raymond Wass, who carried out menial tasks, and had a habit of coming to work in the same unwashed state as when he had left the previous day, This unhygienic habit regularly prompted Hossy and Cocky to throw Raymond in the 'bosh', a steel tank of putrid water used to quench hot forged steel items. Raymond would emerge with hair and clothes dripping wet through, but still had the ever present smile on his face, for he knew he would have a 'breather' from work as he dried himself next to the furnace.

After my alloted time of six months in the Jig and Tool room came to an end Morris gave me a present of a treadle powered wood turning lathe which I installed in our cellar at Wellington Street were I made good use of it by spending many relaxing hours making decorative items, coffee tables and stools. From Jig and Tool I moved to the Foundry, Fitting shop and Wagon assembly line making acquaintance with, and friendship of Tommy Coulson, Eric Ballantyne and Ron Elliott along the way. Special mention must be made of the paint shop foreman Cis Kipling whom with his Wife became good friends of Dad and Mum, introducing them to the then popular craze of attending Stock Car racing at Long Eaton. Cis's working environment was a permanent mist of fine grey paint particles that permeated every pore. As a concession for this hazardous atmosphere he was allowed to consume a free a pint of milk a day. Cis, one of nature's gentlemen died in his early fifties.

The foundry's main output was railway wagon axle boxes manufactured using steel dies supplied by RCH (Railway Clearing House) the organisation responsible for overseeing the procurement for all British Railways rolling stock. The Foundry Manager was Tom Coulson, a quietly spoken and thoughtful metallurgist who in the two short months that I spent with him taught me much about foundry practice and treated me like a son. Eric Ballantyne, a typical RAF pilot type with immaculate Brycream groomed hair and sporting a moustache was the 'dapper' foreman fitter who never ever soiled his Boilersuit. The fitting shops main priority was machine maintenance but they also had a large lathe driven from an overhead shafting and pulley system that was used for final turning of wagon wheel sets. The wagon line assembled the British Railways 16 Ton Steel Mineral Wagon that was the mainstay of their mineral freight business. The wagons were built to RCH specification but many component parts were manufactured to Derbyshire Carriage and Wagon prepared drawings. Specialised wagons, usually ordered in small numbers were the speciality of Ron Elliot, a fabrication plater. I spent two months with Ron working on steel hopper wagons and was taught how to 'develop' (find the correct shape) of plates set at an angle.

In September 1953 I was enrolled at The Chesterfield Technical College to begin study of Mechanical Engineering, commencing at 'Pre-Senior' level. This was a year long foundation course intended for students who had left school without achieving formal qualifications and was a pre-cursor for entry into further study leading to either City and Guilds or National Certificate award. In June of 1954 I sat and passed the examination and my marks qualified me to be selected to study at National Certificate level, which would take a further three years. Three months prior to this John Plackett notified me that my shop floor service had come to an end and on the Tuesday following Easter Monday I would be transferred into the Drawing Office.

It was with great anticipation on that Tuesday morning at just before nine am, dressed in Hacking jacket, shirt, tie and grey flannels that I started to climb the stair way that led to the first floor drawing office. On the small landing mid way up I met a smartly dressed youngish lady descending the stair. Being rather overawed by this new environment I nervously muttered something like good morning and she reciprocated in kind with a more carefree manner and to my utter confusion, in passing placed her hand between my trouser legs and 'groped' me, before carrying on her leisurely journey down the stair. Being just turned sixteen years of age I naturally had occasional fantasies about the anatomy of the opposite sex, and on this occasion as I carried on up the stair and along the corridor to the drawing office; I wasn't sure in my mind whether it had really happened or some figment of my still adolescent yearning. My mind was still in a state of turmoil when I entered the office to be welcomed by Peter Brown, brother-in-law of Cyril Cox, the Chief Draughtsman. Pete, as was his favourite posture, was lounged back on his high swivel chair with feet up on his drawing board and engaged in blowing smoke rings from his Park Drive cigarette. 'Hey up Bry, come in, take a pew' 'Pete, you'll never guess what's just happened!' 'Don't tell me Maureen's baptised you?' So it wasn't a dream then, it really did happen. Pete told me that Maureen, one of the typists, expected to be made a 'fuss' of by the male office staff and particularly enjoyed her breasts being fondled. (Maureen was not her real name). Pete was at that time eighteen years of age, as was the other Junior Draughtsman Derrick Knowles who Pete addressed as Warwick, pronounced as spelt.

The Drawing Office had a distinctive smell, characterised by a combination of linoleum floor covering and diluted ammonia based chemical solution used in the dyeline printer. White five pound notes were still in circulation at that time and Pete was constantly scouring office supplies catalogues seeking an ultra fine printing paper that would reproduce passable counterfeit notes, of course he never succeeded, but not for the want of trying. He also had a wit for words and sayings coming out with such nonsense as; 'I see, said the blind man' and 'There it was gone.' Yes, my book title. He was also an exponent on metamorphose word association. A classic and unique example of his was calling a shilling a 'Roberta' We were discussing in a rather salacious manner a newspaper report on the first transgender operation of a male to a female carried out in this county, the male Robert somebody, or other, became the celebrated female Roberta Cowl. Pete's immediate train of thought was; Roberta-Robert-Bob-Shilling. He was also the consummate raconteur of dirty jokes. One in particular stays fresh in my memory some 55 years after his recital:

There was a young man from Belgrade

Who found a dead Pro in a cave

It took all his pluck to have a cold f..k

But look at the money he saved

Pete also came up with a 'foolproof system' for betting on the William Hill fixed odds football coupon. It went something like this: The Sporting Life Football paper printed all past results of the current season. For the system to work you had to hold off betting until half the season had gone. You would then search for home teams who had beaten their opponents away during the first half of the season. These were your banker homes. Some weeks there would not be any but regularly there would be more than five which was the minimum selection on the coupon. Of course it was not foolproof but I must admit that for two seasons we were ahead of the bookie.

Both Pete and Derrick had recently purchased motor cycles 'on the never never' from Henstocks on Mansfield Road. Pete's pride and joy was a BSA 350cc Gold Star while Derrick had the more pedestrian 250cc C11. To showcase their bikes they visited the youth club I attended, held at the Swanwick Memorial Hall at Old Whittington. On arrival there gathered a crowd of gawping awestruck boys and girls (The word teenager hadn't been formulated then) My two work colleagues took obvious pride in their being the centre of attraction, and wanting to get into the act, and also having a tenuous association, I persuaded Pete to let me ride his bike which he readily and enthusiastically agreed to never considering the risk of me not have a driving licence or insurance, At that time the main road between Old and New Whittington lay between the Revolution House and the Memorial Hall. The now existing sprawling council estate and adjacent bounding road had not as then been built. I took off heading toward New Whittington and was taken aback at the sheer speed attained from very little movement of the throttle twist grip so I steadied off and 'crabbed' my way there and back. Approaching the bend that would take me back to the Memorial Hall I could not resist to show off to the gathered crowd, especially the girls, so leaning the bike over and simultaneously opening the throttle I shot forward and sped out of control for the footrest caught the pavement which caused the bike to flip over and sent me bumping some ten yards along the road. Everything seemed to go in slow motion as I bounced past the gathered crowd and feeling humiliated I picked myself up and tried to put on a convincing brave face as I spurned assistance. Pete's bike had sustained damage to the front folks and wheel but was driveable. As was testament to his generous spirit Pete said; 'don't worry kiddo, I'll soon have it fixed, are you sure you're alright?' As Pete was talking I could feel my socks getting soggy and a warm stinging pain spreading up my legs to my thighs. I began to get light headed and became unsteady. It was lucky for me that someone suggested I be taken across the road to the Church Street premises of Nurse Slinn a practising Midwife as it turned out I was bleeding profusely from severe grazing from my thighs to my ankle bones. My legs still bare the scars that witness that very immature act committed some fifty five years ago.

Talking about motor cycles, Vic Turner, who suffered from a speech impediment that caused him to stutter when excited, was employed as relief machinist and occasional assistant to Harold Garner, the punch machine operator, and was also the pal of Cocky the blacksmith striker. Vic purchased a new 500cc Norton Dominator and on the first day he came to work on it Cocky cadged a lift home. Vic with Cocky riding pillion set off from the main gate heading up South Street and at the first cross road adjacent to the Forge public house a taxi crossed their path. Vic violently swerved to miss the vehicle and was unseated leaving Cocky helpless. The bike careered into the pub wall which resulted in Cocky having his entire front teeth knocked out and suffering also a broken nose. On his return to work some months later he was barely recognisable.

The reader may be thinking that with all this distraction that little work was actually done. On the contrary, Cyril Cox kept a much disciplined office whilst still skilfully managing to have a friendly repartee with his staff. I had at school taken the subject of machine drawing for a period of four years but soon learned under the tuition of Cyril the underlying principles of the technique of good draughtsmanship not encountered at school. Drawings were prepared using pencil on tracing paper then lined in using Indian ink. It took a certain amount of skill to avoid smearing the ink when moving your drawing board parallel square. For all his joie de vivre, Cyril had a penchant of arrogance and intolerance to the shop floor workers, many of whom he treat with distain or sarcasm. I think he was incapable of comprehending that other people had feelings. Typically, he thought it funny to always address Archie Bates, a general labourer, as Master Bates.

Most of our work was in re-drafting 'drawings' supplied by customers to accompany enquiries. Generally the received drawings, in particular those supplied by RCH and NCB (National Coal Board) were of atrocious quality and barely decipherable. The work was interesting and varied but I most enjoyed preparing arrangement drawings of Pit tubs, Mine cars and Man riding cars, all for NCB collieries in North Derbyshire, South Yorkshire and Nottinghamshire

A.F. Pates was the Chairman and Managing Director of the two companies and kept us on our toes by frequent visits to the drawing office as he breezed in like a whirlwind and whilst surreptitiously engaging Cyril on some pretext or other, shot penetrating glances over each drawing board. Frank Pates office was on the ground floor with double aspect widows that gave view of the works yard and front entrance gates on which he kept a constant vigil. The wagon repair shop dealt mainly with wooden bodied railway wagons and when replacing worn out planking were allowed to cut the removed damaged planking into one foot pieces, and be allowed one piece to take home on a Friday afternoon for fire wood. One Friday afternoon a Repairer was going through the gate with his allotted wood tucked underneath his arm which disguised a stolen pot of red lead paint concealed under his coat. Unfortunately the pot slipped and the paint started seeping from under his coat. Instead of carrying on through the gate he stopped to adjust the pot and was seen by Frank, who rushed out into the yard and sacked the hapless character on the spot.

During the spring of 1955 Cyril, who was a heavy smoker, took a routine chest x-ray screening which revealed a shadow on one of his lungs. The treatment and recuperation meant a prolonged stay in hospital, and with the departure of Derrick Knowles some weeks prior, it left Pete and me to 'hold the fort'. As the saying goes; 'The inmates took over the madhouse'. I had just turned seventeen years old and two thirds of the way through the first year proper in Mechanical Engineering at National Certificate level. I was paid a wage of twenty five shillings per week, which before being handed over to me by Bob Woods, the Senior Cashier; I would be interrogated as to what I had done that week to deserve such a large remuneration. I now cannot believe that I stood meekly by his large mahogany desk and recounted in detail my weeks output. Maybe Bob was just a lonely old man and used this as an excuse to give him a little respite from his routinely monotonous job.

Routine and predictable enquiries were quite within our capability and both Pete and I enjoyed the responsibility and freedom that this unexpected change of circumstance had thrown into our laps. This happy state of affairs changed 'slightly' when quite unexpectedly RCH sent an enquiry for the manufacture of fifteen 25 Ton Lowmac Machine Wagons. This was to be a new up rated version of the standard BR 14 Ton Low Machine Wagon which had a well bottom flat platform, and was used for carrying higher than normal items. The new higher rated load version with low floor and small wheels allowed military tracked vehicles, for which it was designed, to be carried within the British loading gauge. The ramps at each end meant that the tracked vehicles could be easily driven on or off. At thirty eight feet long it dwarfed its predecessor and was more than twice the length of the 16 Ton Mineral Wagons then currently being built on the wagon line. RCH had provided a general arrangement drawing showing overall dimensions, and critically, the main frame beams had a curvature peaking at half inch at centre of span. (When a vehicle was loaded onto the wagon its weight would flatten the curvature making the wagon ride level and reduce load on wheel bearings). Frank Pates was desperate to get the order even though it meant an extension of sixty feet to the paint shop located to the rear of the wagon assembly bay which had two common rail tracks with the paint shop. This extension was necessary so as not to compromise the mineral wagon build programme. The Lowmac would be built in tandem by utilising the extra rail accommodation.

Preparing a quotation made an additional time consuming demand on our normal work schedule, and if we won the order this would go exponential with preparation of many detail drawings that would also have to include an elaborate 'exploded' isometric drawing that showed and identified all the separate parts to ensure correct assembly procedure. As if this was not enough to cope with then we were expected to prepare structural drawings details for the proposed paint shop extension.

Frank Pates could not read a drawing and therefore could not grasp the notion of how large and heavy this specialised wagon was to be. The RCH drawing depicted a platform on wheels that appeared on the drawing sheet as about two feet long. It had to be pointed out to him that the four main frame beams, which had to be rolled to a curvature, were actually over thirty feet in length steel joists with a cross section measuring 18 inches by 7 inches and each weighing well over a ton. Frank nevertheless asked me to submit to him a material list breakdown of the wagon to support his quotation and also send a drawing of the curved beam profile to Hadfields Steel Works, Sheffield, to ascertain cost of bending. The quote received from Hadfields was a prohibitive £150 per beam (£600 per wagon set). Frank undaunted by this set back explaining that his son Derek, the Works Manager, would find a way of curving the beams and on this premise he sent RCH a quote that did not include the cost of bending and got the order.

Derek's solution was to clamp the beam to two of the wagon line bay end columns, then heat the centre of the beam with large acetylene torch and pull the beam to the required curvature by using a steel chain attached to the 40 ton overhead crane. Frank Pates asked if I could calculate the pull required by the crane to obtain the required curvature. With my elementary knowledge of beams and bending I came up with a pull of 17 Ton (Ignoring any weakness due to heating as ineffectual due to the size of the beam, in the outside cool atmosphere, losing heat as fast as it was gaining it). I also told him that the beam stiffness (moment of inertia) was twice the value of the two combine columns and as the two twenty feet tall columns were cantilever mounted this pull would deflect these some 18 inches causing the roof to buckle. Derek dismissed this scenario as being flawed and convinced his father that the heat from the large acetylene torch would significantly weaken the beam making bending simple. They went ahead and the whole front of the bay collapsed. The beams were duly dispatched to Hadfields.

I now turned my attention to the paint shop extension that was going to be manufactured and erected by our on site building maintenance foreman Tom

Bradley and his son Alex. Tom, who was a law unto himself, had a small, snug workshop where him and Alex spent most of their time mashing tea on their stove. Ted with ever present flat cap, pipe in mouth, and pencil stub behind ear would regale me with tales of how him and Alex were indispensable to the company. Ted would frequently interject these deeds with 'I'm good, but our Alex is even better.' Alex, who always reminded me of the 'Popeye' cartoon character as his large body bulk never seemed to quite fit inside his bib and brace overalls, oozed confidence that often proved to be unjustified.

Planning of the paint shop extension was a relatively simple exercise it being a 'carbon copy' of the existing paint shop with just one modification. The existing end structure had a centrally placed heavy vertical column, some thirty feet high, running from the floor to the roof ridge and would have to be removed. A ten foot length of the column formed also part of the end roof truss and on removal would be replaced by a light angle iron girder making the truss identical to the other trusses. To ensure that the roof would not be damaged during this operation the truss could not be left in a weak state at any stage of its conversion so I determined that the twenty foot part of the column would be left in situ as a prop whilst the remainder, which weighed quarter of a ton, would be burnt away and replaced by the angle girder. Finally the twenty two foot part of the column would be dismantled leaving the modified truss in situ. I presented a 'before and after' drawing of the truss to Ted and explained in detail the procedure to be carried out. Ted all the while kept interrupting me with; 'Are kid, are kid, I understand,' accompanied by vigorous nodding of his head. Six weeks later Frank Pates requested that I accompany him to view the new extension. I assumed that I would be receiving from him a 'pat on the back' for a job well planned, but as we took up a stance from a distance Frank agitatedly blustered; 'What's that, what's that?' pointing up to the roof of the paint shop. The roof ridges, at a point were the new extension joined the old paint shop, had collapsed forming a 'vee' shaped gulley to the skyline. I could offer no explanation as to why that had occurred until we walked inside and I espied the modified truss still had the ten foot piece of column attached to it, and due to its weight, had caused the local collapse of the roof. Tom had ignored all my procedural instructions and had just separated, by burning, the column in line with the underside of the truss and removed the bottom twenty feet only. My protestations that this was carried out contrary to my explicit instructions fell on deaf ears and my attempt to validate my claim by showing Frank the drawings and instructions issued to Ted Bradley were rebuffed out of hand.

A few weeks earlier Frank Pates had received a panic telephone call from the company transport driver, Harry Jarvis, who was parked outside the gates of Shireoaks Colliery with a lorry load of twenty pit tubs, having been refused entry by the Colliery Manager who would not accept the delivery as one of the tubs had some sort of fault. Not wanting to incur additional transportation costs Frank instructed Harry to stay putt and he would dispatch someone to 'sort' it out; that someone was me accompanied by the company representative and salesman, Charlie Solly who was to drive me there. On arrival we were confronted by an intimidating figure of a man, who later reminded me of Eugene 'Bull' Connor the Public Safety Commissioner of Birmingham, Alabama whose demonstration of racial intolerance to members of the Civil Rights Movement during there marches in the 1960's made news headlines the world over. This characters first word were; 'Are you two effers from Whittington Engineering?' and not waiting for reply continued with the command; I'm the Pit Manager, follow me.' We three went up to the lorry and the Manager, who never told me his name, pointed out a tub that had got a six inch square steel patch protruding from of its sides. 'See that carbuncle, if you ordered a new car and it came with paint runs and a patch on its door, would you accept it?' As I shook my head he went on;' its shoddy and hazardous, now get out of my sight.'

Now I knew that the width of a pit tub had to be a precise size so has to fit snugly into the shaft cage to minimise the risk of any movement between the two that may creating sparks with consequent danger of fire, so real diplomacy would be needed to rescue the situation. I apologised profusely in an undignified grovelling manner and appealing to his good nature by pointing out our previous good relations, finally offering to get a workman and tackle on site immediately to rectify the problem. To my and Charlie's amazement the Manager 'reluctantly' accepted, and with that his mood changed becoming most pleasant even to offering us a cup of tea. On the way back to Whittington Charlie kept saying; 'Brian I don't know how you pulled it off.' For us both realised that we had averted a crisis that may have led to the company being removed from NCB tender lists. We were on an adrenalin rush and real 'chuffed' with our selves as we reported back to Frank Pates. On hearing my concession and promise to rectify the tub Frank exploded with an angry threat to renege on the promise and shouting in my face; I'm the boss, I make all the decisions, you have no authority to go behind my back. When Frank finally calmed down he asked me to debrief Ray Fiddler on the nature of what the work involved then Ray was dispatched with tool box, burning gear and welding machine loaded on back of the pickup truck

When Jimmy Greaves was asked why the tub had a patch he had no knowledge of it. It turned out that Gil Hibbert was training a young lad to be a burner and instructed him to go out into the stockyard and find a piece of scrap plate from which he should burn a test piece that should be a square of six inches by six inches. Unbeknown to Gil the lad had chosen to burn the square out of the centre of a large plate that had been order in as part of the Shireoaks order. These tub assemblies were supervised by Les Wheatcroft who authorised the welding a patch on the tub side to cover the burnt hole. Les hadn't the gumption to even have the patch on the inside of the tub which of course would still have been unacceptable but at least the tub would have fitted into the cage. Ray Fiddler burned off the patch and welded in flush, a square of the same gauge plate as the tub. The welding was also ground flush and the area repainted. Including the travelling time it took less than half a day and went a long way in restoring the Manager's faith of the integrity of Whittington Engineering

Frank Pates vitriolic and unjustified outburst led me to believe that I did not view my long term future being spent at Whittington Engineering, and the later roof truss debacle strengthen my resolve to leave the company as soon as possible. To that end on 25th August of 1955 I applied for a position as a Staff Apprentice Draughtsman within the Aero Engine Division of Rolls-Royce Ltd., and was invited for interview at Derby on the 31st August. I was interviewed by Ron Kibby, the Chief Draughtsman who at the end of the interview informed me that I had been successful and was invited to join the company on Monday 3rd October.

As a matter of courtesy I forewarned Frank Pates via John Placket of my intension of leaving the company at the end of the month and was immediately summoned into his presence. 'Now what's all this nonsense? Don't be big headed, go back upstairs and I'll forget it.' I do believe in his arrogance that he thought it was a bluff tactic on my part.

Peter Brown booked a foursome weekend away at Blackpool Illuminations at the latter part of September to; 'Celebrate my liberation from Serfdom' Also going were Pat Bartholomew and Marion Bullas two girls from the Comptometer Department. Pat, whose parents kept a shop in Eckington, was eighteen months older than me and hinted that I may be on a 'Promise' that weekend. Knowing Pat's nature of displaying overt bravado in front of the other girls, then reneging at the last minute I was counting on it happening, but I was holding my breath. Pat viewed her role as some sort of Pied Piper to the rest of the girls, where she went the rest followed like giggling sheep. One morning Pete had a button come off his trouser fly. (There were no zips fitted in them days). As soon as Pat got wind of this she, closely followed by girls, came up to the

Drawing Office and made an unsolicited offer to sew it back on. Pete gave her the button and she retired promising to come back with needle and thread. As we waited in anticipation the time seemed to drag but then Pat, accompanied by the girls, made her appearance brandishing the needle with button dangling on the thread. Pete nonchalantly lay back on his chair and spread is legs inviting Pat to proceed. There was short standoff before Pat blushingly left the stage.

We four caught an early morning train to Blackpool and spent the afternoon at Bloomfield Road watching Stanley Matthews playing football for Blackpool. The early evening was spent in the Manchester Hotel were the girls kept ordering Pimm's cocktails at a shilling a glass. Eventually the table supported a pyramid of empty tumblers some two feet high. A local photographer took a snapshot of the four of us sat facing this pyramid and each of us received a copy. Unfortunately my photo is lost. Pat have you still got yours? With much badgering we persuaded the girls to take leave of the Manchester Hotel and cross the promenade to the beach. This short journey was really the only time I viewed the illuminations. As we were approaching the Central Pier who's under structure was in deep shadow the girls feigned tiredness due to the excitement of the afternoon football and too many Pimm's, and requested that we escort them back to the B&B. I knew it, I knew it.

It wasn't yet ten o'clock so Pete and I made our way to the Winter Gardens were we fell in with six 'Old Dears' from Newcastle who was out on a 'Jolly'. Trying to impress them that we were; 'Men about Town' we offered to buy them a drink. Five were drinking Milk Stout, and the one who was making a fuss of me, was on Guinness. Acting the gallant gentleman I offered to pour the drink out for her and never ever having poured a Guinness out in my life embarrassingly proceeded to fill the glass with just a frothy head that overflowed onto the table. She took me to the bar and ordered another bottle of Guiness then demonstrated to me how to successfully pour it from the bottle to the glass by acutely tilting both then gently straightening the glass. Now whenever I pour out a fizzy drink I have fond memories of that Saturday night in the Winter Gardens.

I departed Whittington Engineering amicably taking with me only the fondest memories and nostalgically still retain them. My new career at Rolls-Royce though posing different challenges would prove to be just as fruitful as regards meeting odd characters and their scams, and I look forward to penning the next volume; 'Yea Old Wine Brewers' the story of my time at Rolls-Royce, marriage and family up to 1971 Talking of family my closing chapter is a special dedication to my Mother who sadly passed away some four years ago and is sorely missed.

Chapter 17 – Family Affairs

Yet each man kills the thing he loves,

By each let this be heard,

Some do it with a bitter look,

Some with a flattering word,

The coward does it with a kiss,

The brave man with a sword!

OSCAR WILDE

The Ballad of Reading Gaol

Mum on the occasion of her 18th Birthday

My maternal grandmother's forebears the Listers were no great shakes when it came to physical attractiveness. This trait would be passed down through the generations to my own time. Often I am told 'You ain't no oil painting, are you.' Being darn right ugly, I have no defence to this allegorical statement but paradoxically a photograph of my Mum taken on the occasion of her eighteenth birthday in 1933 shows a serene beauty whose enigmatic smile rivals that of the Mona Lisa. It was thought that Hilda's future prospects of a secure and happy future was assured as her attractive appearance was not her only attribute for she was also the eldest daughter of Walter Hardy a successful motor car dealer who had the respect of the Chesterfield social and business communities. Alas, within a few short months of her coming of age a single brief indiscretion would turn Mums life upside down bringing shame upon herself and her family and then tragedy to this young woman the turmoil of which would blight her life.

Friday nights were mine and Mums special time. Dad had 'gone to the dogs' at Wheeldon Mill a greyhound racing stadium. Bernard my elder brother was out playing in the street and in later years on the town with his friend Ray Brownlow aka 'Bambo.' I would help Mum to make my favourite jam tarts and whilst they were baking we would cuddle up with a cuppa and listen to the radio or just talk away the hours. In later years we would regularly go to the Lyceum cinema on Whittington Moor were she would, from sheer exhaustion, drop fast asleep even in the middle of *The Gunfight at the OK Corral* were her loud snoring easily drowned out the action.

Even at my early age Mum often spoke to me of our Beryl, my half sister who had died of pneumonia and whooping-cough shortly after her second birthday in 1936. Mum told me the father of our Beryl was the son of a Pottery owner at New Whittington were she was then working in 1933. She said 'I was asked to stay behind one evening by the owner's son to help him finish some work.'

She did not confide his name. She then continued 'There was only the two of us and as the evening wore on he asked me to go in the inner office for a tea break' She told me she did not feel at all uneasy as he had always been the perfect gentleman. My Mum then claimed 'He forcibly raped me.' I reserve any moral judgement, as in later life my Mum recollections were coloured like those of Blanche Dubois in *A Streetcar Named Desire*. She would always say to me 'I was born to be a Lady, but got chucked on the wrong heap.' There is some evidence that this veneer of being a lady gave suspicion of a promiscuous past. The bare facts are that as consequence, our Beryl was the issue of this brief union being born in March 1934.

One incident that was never resolved in my mind occurred in the summer of 1946. Proctors Funfair was making a period visit to Stand Road Park which was occasion of great excitement for us kids with its appetising smell of hotdogs, loud music, lights, stalls, sideshows and of course the rides such as Noah's Arc, Dodgems, Aerial Chairs and Waltzer. It was a Friday night and as usual Dad had gone to the dog track at Wheeldon Mill whilst Mum took Esme, Bernard and me to the fair. It had already been an eventful evening as Claytons, a rival travelling family to the Proctors, had unexpectedly arrived and set up their fair a little way up the park. The two families and their working gangs had 'squared up to each other' before calling a truce and the two fairs agreed to co-exist. It had been quite a frightening experience for the fair going public but soon it was forgotten amid the noise and excitement. We had been on the fair about two hours when Dad made an unexpected early appearance. He was in a rage and took Mum by the hair then dragged her back to Devonshire Street, leaving our Es to get me and Bernard safely home. There had been a few minor incidents in the past, but Dad had never before been abusive to Mum, in fact he had a very placid nature, so it must have been something very serious to cause him to react in this violent manner.

In 1930s Britain, and in fact, right up to the end of the 1950s, a female who was unfortunate to have a baby out of wedlock was vilified and pilloried as a fallen woman, by hypocritical pillars of society, who took great delight out of someone's misfortune. Worse for the unfortunate recipient was the unbearable guilt she had to bear for inflicting the associated shame on her parents and extended family. Mum said 'I felt emotionally and physically drained as all the sneers were led by my dear Aunt Gert' (Gertrude Lister, wife of Bernard and matriarch of the two extended families). In 1935, this stigma far from being forgiven, or forgotten, was perceived by the Hardy and Lister clans to be compounded, when Hilda married below their own expectations to a person with no ambition and little prospect, my father Walter Ellis.

My Mum was perversely isolated within her own family and her natural maternal instinct was to draw even closer to her infant daughter. To my question 'What was she like.' Her reply was 'Your sister was a beautiful lively and mischievous baby who gave out her love to everyone.' 'She was oblivious to the bigotry and heartache of her surroundings.' 'Mum, why did we lose her?' She answered 'At first she was flushed and grizzly and had a slight cough that disturbed her sleep, the cough got worse during the night so I sent for the doctor, who thought it was just a chill on her lungs and just to keep her wrapped up warm' In my childish naive way I asked 'Is that all he did, could he not cure her with some medicine?' Mum did not reply but broke down into an uncontrollable sobbing fit. I still cannot after all these years forget that feeling of deep sorrow emanating from her very soul. After a time she said 'I nursed her for three days and nights, each day I witnessed her suffering getting worse with the incessant coughing. In desperation Mum again sent for the doctor who diagnosed Whooping-Cough and inflammation of the lungs caused by abscesses. He arranged for Beryl's immediate removal to hospital. My Mum was in constant attendance and described her feelings at that time to me 'As her mother I felt devastated and completely helpless hearing her exhausted cries as she was fighting for breath between violent convulsions and that constant hacking cough.' Then Mums worse nightmare began when our Beryl developed full blown Pneumonia. For a further two days and nights Beryl fought for her very existence with her helpless and drained Mum never leaving her side. My Mum with tears in her eyes told me 'When her little lungs gave up I though it was a blessing that her pain was ended but I am racked with guilt that God took her from me and made my innocent baby pay for my sins.' In the early thirties diphtheria, tuberculosis along with pneumonia and whooping cough were rampant and infant mortality was common occurrence. In our own street in the 1940s I was aware of three such juvenile deaths among my peer group.

Beryl was interred in the grave yard of St Johns Church, Newbold. She would welcome and share her resting place with another infant girl, who also died of pneumonia forty six years later. She was our first born child Dawn Mahala. No, my wife and I do not believe in the saying;' The sins of the parents are visited on their children.' On the contrary, we by sharing a common tragedy, feel that we have come to understand her suffering and therefore have empathy with my extraordinary Mum.

Yes my Mum had steely determination with strength of character that saw me through a difficult first two years of life. Whilst working at a full time day job and two evenings a week she managed to keep the house spotless clean and feed and clothe the both of us. Early or later Mum would always tuck us up in bed and kiss us goodnight. Every Friday Mum would buy me and Bernard a comic, cartwheel biscuit and sweets. Saturday's she would buy us a lead toy soldier from the Chesterfield market. Mum made sure that I had good books to read such as Masterman Ready, The Coral Island, The Water Babies, Kidnapped and Treasure Island. I still have these books. It was Mum who fought tooth and nail with Dad to let me attend Junior Technical School were a school uniform was mandatory instead of the non uniformed Secondary Modern School that was

Dads preference. Mum had to scrub floors for over three months to buy that uniform of cap, blazer, tie, two grey shirts, two pairs of short grey trousers, four pairs of grey woollen socks, black leather shoes, two white vests, gym shorts, pumps and a leather satchel. On my first day at school someone stole my tie from the gymnasium changing room. I cried in indignant rage to think that Mum had worked three days for that tie and it would have to be replaced. Mum accompanied me to Derby and gave me moral support for my forthcoming interview as a staff apprentice with Rolls-Royce Ltd., where I subsequently progressed within the company to the appointment of Aero Engine Design Engineer.

My wife Barbara was more of a daughter than daughter-in-law to Mum and she also had a very special relationship with Dad, something that I personally could never achieve. With Barbara's initiation and financial assistance obtained through working full time nights at Walton Hospital I was able to train to become a school teacher at the Matlock Campus of Nottingham University. There was once again discord between me and Dad as he vigorously disagreed with my decision to leave Rolls-Royce but Barbara and Mum persuaded him to back down.

With my graduation in June of 1975 I took up a Mathematics teaching post at Poltair School St Austell Cornwall. We, as a then family of five, had been in Cornwall just two weeks when my Father died suddenly. My Mum insisted that we did not make the long journey back for my Dads funeral as she thought it unsettling for our boys. I regret to this day that I did not get to say goodbye to Dad but I am sure Mum made the right judgement Yes, my Mum was extraordinary, but more importantly she was a devoted, and loving mother to her two sons.

Prelude

1933 – 1938

In terms of historic significance the year of my birth 1938 was a momentous year. There was a distinct probability of Great Britain, yet again, being drawn into a war with Germany, just twenty years after the armistice of the Great War, due to Germany's annexation of Austria in March. Throughout the year the BBC news reported demand after demand for a Greater Germany, at the expense of smaller European countries, by Adolf Hitler, the German Chancellor, causing fear and anxiety in the minds of the British public. This trepidation was somewhat alleviated when in September the British Prime Minister, Neville Chamberlain's returned from Munich having secured an agreement of understanding with Herr Hitler. He was shown by cinema newsreels at the time, waving a piece of paper of this agreement, which he said 'Meant peace in our time.' This brought about great relief to the public who viewed him has a saviour of the country. One year later Great Britain was at war with Germany.

Of more general interest, it was the year that the steam locomotive, Mallard, set a world speed record for steam locomotives, reaching a peak speed of 126mph. Graham Green wrote *Brighton Rock*. Errol Flynn starred in the swashbuckling film *The Adventures of Robin Hood*. The popular hit tune, *Thanks for the Memory*, became American comedian Bob Hope's enduring theme song after he introduced it on The Big Broadcast of 1938.

Political, cultural and social events of 1938 dominated by the increasing threat of war with Germany certainly influenced the mood of the nation in Britain to a greater or lesser extent. For a significant group of the populace faced with abject poverty of unemployment or low paid unskilled labour, these events must have barely registered on their cognitive thoughts which were fully occupied elsewhere with the anxiety of finding the means to provide the family with their next meal. The lack of a welfare state was the major factor which precluded the government from offering little more than token financial assistance to this poor and needy social group.

In the first month of 1938 my family was typical of that group. Walter and Hilda Ellis, my parents, together with Bernard Walter, their eighteen month old son were then lodging in one room at 14 Manknell Road, a house tenanted by Walter's parents with four of their children. The overcrowded conditions prevented privacy and decency, in every respect. Hilda, in particular was subject to constant embarrassment with constant violation of their small space. To add pressure into this intolerable stressful cauldron, there would soon to be an additional mouth to feed. Hilda was expecting her second child in a few weeks time.

Walter was employed by Bradshaw's Pottery, one of many potteries scattered around Chesterfield, on a casual basis, as a jobbing labourer, stacking unglazed wares into Beehive kilns and emptying kilns of fired wares. His weekly income of £1 10s 0d was low and irregular, about a third of average wage. To supplement this low income he would, on a regular weekly basis, walk from Whittington Moor to Chesterfield, often with Bernard perched on his shoulders to attend the dole office where he was submitted to a means review, and if he qualified, he would receive a sum of half a crown (two shillings and sixpence). Often there was no money forthcoming. It was into this environment that I was born on 4th February 1938.

It may be construed, by the reader, that this young couple had acted in the most irresponsible and deplorable manner in exposing such young children to such deprivation. In fact, conditions and circumstances prevailing during the previous decade had conspired against them. And fate did the rest;

At the time of their marriage, in December 1935, Walter was twenty two years old. He was the eldest of six children born to Percy and Mahala Ellis (nee Orwin). Other siblings were: Percy, Wilfred, Raymond, May and Ethel. His father was a labourer employed by Staveley Coal & Iron Company. His grandfather, Charles Ellis, also worked at Staveley as a fitter. Walter's occupation was a journeyman potter, being employed by Bradshaws pottery. He had a regular weekly income of £ 2 2s 0d.

Hilda was twenty years old. She was the eldest of five children born to Walter and Mary Ellen Hardy (nee Lister). Other siblings being: John Walter (Jack), Sidney, Joan and Esme. Her father was in business as a second hand motor car and scrap metal dealer. Hilda did not have outside employment, but assisted her mother in household duties. .

Hilda's grandparents, George and Elizabeth Lister (nee Cain) had ten, possibly eleven, children, her mother was third born. George had been a miner in his early years before purchasing a grocery and off-licence shop, combined with living premises, at the junction of Arundel Road and Mountcastle Street during the First World War.

My grandfather Walter Hardy had also began his working life as a miner, but on his marriage to Mary Ellen, had began working for his father in law as a costermonger, selling wet fish from a barrow. Hilda often accompanied her father.

In the 1920s, Walter Hardy's brother in law, Bernard Lister, had established a scrap metal business, trading from a tenanted site at Dunston Road. The land owner was The Duke of Devonshire's Chatsworth Estates. With the growth of his business, now incorporating sales of motor cars and spares, in the late 1920s, he first employed Walter Hardy as a motor mechanic, then offered Walter the tenancy as he was re-locating to larger premises at Sheepbridge.

Walter by 1935 had built up a successful and profitable business by utilising the ethos of Bernard Lister, and he was able to employ his two sons Jack and Sidney in a full time capacity.

The Hardy's, a respected family, with creditable status within the business community of Chesterfield in 1933, must have been devastated with the news that Hilda was pregnant. The child, a girl, was born in March 1934, and christened Beryl Hardy. Tragically, the infant died of pneumonia and whooping-cough shortly after her second birthday. In the early thirties diphtheria, tuberculosis along with pneumonia and whooping cough were rampant and infant mortality was common occurrence.

In 1935, this stigma far from being forgiven, or forgotten, was perceived by the Hardy and Lister clans to be compounded, when Hilda married below their own expectations to a person with no ambition and little prospect. This bigotry, orchestrated by Gertrude Lister, wife of Bernard and Matriarch of the two extended families, created a festering undercurrent of recrimination, blighting family relationships, extending to generations yet unborn, and exists to this day.

Reminds one of John Galsworthy's epic trilogy The Forsyte Saga, albeit, on a less grandeur stage.

After their marriage, Walter and Hilda rented a bed sitting room at number 12 St Johns Road. Whilst residing there, their first child, a boy, Bernard Walter, was born at the Chesterfield Royal Hospital on 14 July 1936.

Around that time Walter secured employment with B R Mills Transport, as a lorry driver. He had held a driving licence since 1931 which stated 'Hereby licence to drive a Motor Vehicle of any class or description'. The vehicle assigned to him was a 1924 Leyland 20 cwt Subsidy Model flat bed lorry, with cab sides open to the elements, wooden bench seat, and rudimentary leaf spring suspension, that I can testify, made it a real bone shaker. With its original brass carbide side and head lamps, and hand painted chocolate brown livery, it really had seen better days. His wages at £2.15s 4d a week was an improvement on what Bradshaw's had been paying.

In May of 1937 Mills took up a contract from the Ministry of Defence, the requirement of which was to supply four vehicles plus drivers to haul barrage balloons, search lights, ack, ack anti aircraft guns, ancillary equipment and stores and provisions, to and from designated sites located on the Yorkshire coast at the resort town of Filey. This exercise was initiated due to the prevailing tension in Europe. The Time period was to be determined by the course of events. It would mean living in a tented area within the main army compound at Filey, for the duration. Walter was one of the delegated drivers. He was given no option. He was informed there were plenty on the dole queue, who would jump at the chance. The sweetener was the expected rate of pay was £3.3s 0d for the seven day working week. Home visits would be infrequent. You could visualise the soul searching of this couple with the prospect of long periods of separation, but the alternative was a return to the dole queue. Walt was eventually to spend a miserable six months at Filey before the MoD closed down the civil requirement of the operation in November 1937. There is no doubt that it was a most dispiriting and miserable time for Walter, and the heavily pregnant Hilda, struggling to cope with the loneliness, irregular payments of money from Mills, and bringing up a child on her own. Testament is extracts from letters written at the time and reproduced below verbatim:

Extract from letter post mark 21st July 1937

Dear Hilda

Im Sorry I could'nt drop a Letter sooner as we have been up side down this is Monday 9PM had a right blow out, we have been running all over the show. Job is easy but its hours and finding your way about well kid I hope you are well and send a letter as soon as possible as I am longing to know how Bunty is

Mr Mills is coming back Thursday and I may be able to let you know when we shall be in but I think it will be sunday I am ready I'll tell you Well this is Pay ticket form 7 days 3 – 3 - 0

Less rations 1s a day 7 – 0

Insurance 1 – 7

Home 1 – 10 – 0

I got at Camp Sun 1 – 4 – 5

Well Hilda according to your letter our Bunt must be keeping OK that's a lot. I think of him times many a day and you as you know it seems very funny being away from you so long but it will soon be over now . I fully expected a letter Saturday Morning but there was on for all but me and I know Baby wants looking after god bless him

The letter is trying to explain that he is seldom in main camp but travelling around satellite sites. He is worried that if a letter arrives whilst he is away from main camp it will be mislaid. He is also trying to explain why the money sent home is not as much as had promised, Mills never made mention of stoppages. Bunt or Bunty is his pet name for his son Bernard. The number columns are money and read as Pounds, Shillings and Pence. Typically entered as £3 3s 0p.

Extract from letter post marked 7th August 1937

Well kid Im enclosing a 10/- Postal Order as I thought Mills would have left you at least £2 and you know you can have every meg of mine for the asking so if that not enough just drop a quick line and you'll have it straight away up to every penny as ive still got about 12/- left.

Money shortage was always a problem. Mr Mills was very cavalier about delivery to Hilda. The numbers are old shillings.

Extract from letter post mark some time in October 1937

Dear Hilda

I got your parcel & letter the parcel land first I opened it and hunted high and low for a letter or a note I was dissappointed when I could'nt find one I thought it was over, and I did, nt intend writing any more well about half hour he brought me the letter and to cut it short I was pleased

This extract encapsulates the nature of their precarious relationship at that time. Walter was convinced that Hilda was about to leave the marital home.

Their relief at being re-united was short lived by the action of Mills temporarily laying Walter off work in mid November, due to termination of MoD contract. He was then offered menial work, on a casual basis by his former employer, Bradshaws, which was gratefully accepted. This reduction of income meant vacating St Johns Road and re-locating to Manknell Road just before Christmas. The New Year was fast approaching, bringing with it, the arrival of another baby. A short time after my birth Dad was re-employed by B R Mills and we moved into our first home at 20 Devonshire Street.

Brian Roger Ellis
Family Tree Information

Brian Ellis – Paternal Grandparents:

Percy Ellis born 1891 married Mahala Orwin born 1892
Married on 23rd December 1911
Percy then age 20 resided at 31 Haywood Street, Brimington –
Occupation Crabman
Fathers name Charles Ellis – Occupation Fitter (Stavely Works)
Mahala then age 19 resided at 159 Scarsdale Road, Whittington Moor
Fathers name William Orwin – Occupation – Fettler

Brian Ellis – Maternal Grandparents:

Walter Hardy born 1891 married Mary Ellen Lister born 1895
Married on 11th April 1914
Walter then age 23 resided at 5 Arundal Road, Newbold Moor –
Occupation Miner
Fathers name Alban Hardy – Occupation Miner
Mary Ellen then age 19 resided at 59 Mountcastle Street, Newbold Moor
Fathers name George A Lister born 1859 – Occupation Miner

Brian Ellis – Parents:

Walter Ellis born 28th February 1913
Hilda Ellis (nee Hardy) born 2nd April 1915
Married 14th December 1935.

Barbara Ellis (*nee Woodward*)

Family Tree Information

Parents:

Thomas James Woodward born 1893
Patience Hunt born 1892

Married 23rd February 1913

Thomas James age 20 resided at Whittington –
Occupation Fireman (Furnace Stoker)
Fathers name Thomas Woodward – Occupation Head Furnace Man
Mothers name Mary.
Thomas and Mary – Daughter born 10th February 1895 christened
Beatrice May Woodward.

Patience age 21 resided at Whittington
Fathers name George Hunt – Occupation Insurance Agent

Barbara:

Born 9th January 1939

Married Brian Roger Ellis 10th June 1961

Children – Dawn Mahala born 11th March 1962
Andrew Richard born 4th May 1963
Simon David born 5th January 1965
Jason Mark born 14th October 1969
Christian James Walter born 27th September 1976